casa americana

THANK YOU.
Paula Acosta
03-26-04

Agrait-Betancourt Alcock Anelli Andrade/Morettin Barney-Caldas
Bozas Browne Clusellas/Baliero Dahl-Rocha De la Guardia/Victoria
Echeverri González de León Iglesia Jiménez
Kalach Laguinge Larrañaga/Obadía
Loreto Mendes da Rocha Peláez ■ TEN

casa americana

Selected and introduced by
Enrique Larrañaga

Birkhäuser – Publishers for Architecture
Basel • Boston • Berlin

Originally published in 2003 under the title
casa americana

Original Spanish version *Tanais Ediciones s.a., (Seville, Madrid)*
English edition *Birkhäuser – Publishers for Architecture (Basel)*
Italian edition *Logos (Modena)*

Publisher *Raúl Rispa*
Executive Editor *Valeria Varas*

Selection and introductory essay *Enrique Larrañaga*

Original drawings, plans, photographs and texts of the 21 works
The architects, their teams and collaborators (see pages 3
and 168 ff.)

English Editor *Teresa Santiago*
English translation by *Gavin Powell*
Text editing by *Lettice Small*
Design and Layout by *Natalia Billotti / equipo editorial Tanais*

A CIP catalogue record for this book is available from the Library
of Congress, Washington D.C., USA

Bibliographic information published by
Die Deutsche Bibliothek
Die Deutsche Bibliothek lists this publication
in the Deutsche Nationalbibliografie;
detailed bibliographic data is available
in the Internet at <http://dnb.ddb.de>

© Tanais Ediciones, s.a., 2003
© 2003 for this English edition:
 Birkhäuser – Publishers for Architecture, P.O. Box 133
 CH-4010 Basel, Switzerland

Member of the BertelsmannSpringer Publishing Group

This work is subject to copyright. All rights are reserved, whether the
whole or part of the material is concerned, specifically the rights of
translation, reprinting, re-use of illustrations, recitation, broadcast-
ing, reproduction on microfilms or in other ways, and storage in
data banks. For any kind of use, permission of the copyright owner
must be obtained.

Colour separation
Proyectos Gráficos Digitales, s.a.
Printed by Agrupem, Madrid
Printed on acid-free paper produced from chlorine-free pulp. TCF∞

Printed in Spain

ISBN: 3-7643-6958-2
D.L.: M-10568-2003

9 8 7 6 5 4 3 2 1

www.birkhauser.ch

6	Autobiographies of a Place: America and the Realisation of Utopia Enrique Larrañaga
16	Gerazzi House Mendes da Rocha
24	LE House TEN
32	Caracola House Browne
38	Horas Claras House Peláez
46	Lott House Jiménez
54	House in La Barranca de San Isidro Dahl-Rocha
62	House in Córdoba Laguinge
68	Floridia House De la Guardia / Victoria
74	House in La Barranca Clusellas / Baliero
82	House on the Lake Agrait Betancourt
90	House in Las Lomas de la Lagunita Larrañaga / Obadía
98	La Queja House Barney-Caldas
104	Casabe House Loreto
110	D'Alessandro House Andrade / Morettin
118	House on the banks of the River Paraná Iglesia
126	House at the Paulinia dam Anelli
132	Posada House Echeverri
138	Amsterdam House González de León
146	La Ribereña Alcock
154	La Reina House Boza
160	Negro House Kalach
168	The Authors

Autobiographies of a Place: America and the Realisation of Utopia

Enrique Larrañaga

It is difficult to define what we are, but our works speak for us. Octavio Paz

In 1498, when Christopher Columbus first sighted the eastern coast of the land which would later be called Venezuela, convinced that he was approaching the Earthly Paradise, the West embarked upon a so far unfinished journey towards the possible. As in a magic mirror which entwines memories and desires nurtured among voluptuous mountains which penetrate the sea, the present contains traces of a past which, as in the Utopia later dreamed of by Thomas More, unveils the future like a promise and thus shows us History as a programme and not only as a procession of events.

The traces of this call to freedom in the modern project make the arrival in America, not merely a political, economic and religious process, but also a radical mutation of western culture, which then initiated the process of plans and hopes which still embraces and concerns us. It is therefore not groundless to assert that modernity is a project with American nationality, founded in the conviction that it is possible, or perhaps essential, to create Utopia, both to fulfil its promise and to understand fully its sense and purpose. This has been the intention and driving force behind the construction of the American world. Utopia is ever in the process of being imagined, fashioned, texted and revised in the far from easy, sometimes accidental but always agitated process of searching. It blends the visions of the peoples who arrived in these lands in search of a promise or those who arrived in chains as slaves toiling but still searching. And all confronted by adverse conditions, stirring landscapes, cruel dramas and intense exchanges.

The adventurer who set off to seek his fortune eventually came face to face with the reality that it is almost always easier to leave than to return and that the land he went to in search of life would, in the end, be witness to his death. Challenged by the urgency of his task and suppressing, by sheer willpower, any longing for the home he had left behind, he opened roads, founded cities and built houses which, though improvised and provisional, made his banishment easier to bear. With memory as a sextant, he appealed to the images which custom had planted in his mind and set about the construction of the new world using the co-ordinates of the world he had left behind, only to discover that what is remembered is rarely what really occurred.

For the migrants who shaped the new continent did not break completely with the land they left behind, but neither did they simply transpose their customs onto a different context. Faced with fears of the immediate future, and through a process of complex adaptation, adjustments and even mutations, they induced the transmigration of known spirits into unwonted bodies which were thus animated by different forces, interwoven echoes and metaphorical presences. The black melancholy which entwines with the fatalism of gypsy singing in the sweet heart-rending tones of the bolero; the mixes of skins, eyes, hair, lips and flesh in the features of the American; leaves, lands, salts and blazing sunshine enhancing the flavour of dishes which blend the Spanish, the Indian and the Negro; or the syncretism of indigenous icons, African rites and Christian principles in a fabulous everyday reality—all combined to build the harmonious heterogeneity which consistently and almost subliminally animates the American tradition in abstractions and juxtapositions that are complex and simultaneous.

Paz, Octavio, In *Search of the Present*

Abstraction as a method enlaces the real and the ideal, transforming rigid models into flexible principles which thus transmigrate into the recognisable but autonomous soul of a presence without nostalgia; on the

Although American urban planning tends to be attributed to the Laws of the Indies, these were promulgated in 1573 and then published in 1681, after the majority of the American cities of the colonial era had already been founded.

Architects such as Antonio Bonet in Argentina, Manuel Mujica Millan in Venezuela, Tomas Auñon in the Dominican Republic, Felix Candela in Mexico and, later on, Max Cetto, Lina Bo Bardi, Artur Kahn or Leopoldo Rother, to name but a few, had a significant influence on American architecture of the mid-20th century, infusing it with its definitive modern expression.

other hand, juxtaposition as a system opens up this presence to the simultaneous and allows it to observe, explore, celebrate and appropriate dissonance and contrast as entity and identity.

The design of the nascent cities, drawn up in accordance with a private map, gave concrete form to the memory of native villages which no longer existed. But its implementation lacked both prior agreement and explicit programming which coincided only in a dream. The American house, with the rigour of its simple geometry, attaches absolute value to the specific mood of the house and the Andalusian farmstead which it evokes. The native baroque of the Paraguayan Missions, the cheerful church towers of Tlaxcala, the mulatto rococo of Ouro Preto, the dense balconies and doorways in Lima of the Mannerism School or the vibrant colour of popular architecture, transform the accidental into emancipation. Among archetypal forms which merge the everyday with the sacred and synchronous strata of superimposed presences, abstraction and juxtaposition intensify the essential, thereby assimilating it into an inclusive everyday affair.

From an order sustained by suitably distilled memories and free accessibility to the diverse, American popular architecture proposes simple but effective mechanisms of spatial intervention between rooms and scales to give form to the situations which constitute the human world and to institute its cycles. Customary hallways, deep windows, wide passageways, vibrant colours and forceful tectonics combine in an architecture which mixed affectionately with the land, permeable in space but lacking experience and which, with simplicity, humility and forcefulnes entertained, at least in its early years, the promise of a possible space.

Sadly, with the passing years the imaginative intensity of those days of interwoven transmigrations, of liberating inclusiveness and hybrid joy lessened, until it was confined to a routine of exclusion and drugged misery struggling under the illusion of magic and myths. That open society of adventurers which was capable of begetting the libertarian euphoria of the early 19th century evolved into a succession of voracious *caudillos*, fratricidal fighting and aberrant marginalisation which tore at the promise, almost destroying it in the process. Recovering the challenge as a plan, modernity gives back to these lands their desire for utopia. The refreshing vitality of the verses of Rubén Darío, the telluric power of Mexican muralism, the sensual materiality of the gardens of Roberto Burle-Marx (Brazil), the ancestral simplicity of the works of Joaquín Torres-García (Uruguay), the clear, strong lines of the buildings of Antonio Vilar in Argentina, Emilio Duhart in Chile or Mario Romañach in Cuba, to name but a few, and the undeniable breath of fresh air provided by the forced migrations stemming from the European wars, restored energy which seemed to have faded and made the possible once again necessary.

With passion as a weapon, the imagination as a challenge and necessity once again converted into opportunity, the American soul and its architecture have once more taken up exploration as the reason behind a project which uses the truth of the material, the presence of tradition and the form of the territory in a renewed attempt to realise Utopia.

An Inquiry into Matter
If the discourse on Iberian architecture helps to intensify its intrinsic honesty, America then assumes as an ontological principle the methodological rule to make physical veracity a manifestation of metaphysical truth. Like the houses in Angostura, built on, between, with, and from stones to manifest the world, the evident material nature of all tangible objects, and the immanent materiality which reveals the world as an experience, all mingle to affirm the profound unity between the physical and the essential and thereby construct the world from those elements which, as presences of the general order, celebrate it almost as if the truth had been transformed into matter.

Ethically, this material truth constructs the real sense and the real wealth of things, beyond their finiteness, as in the house where Juvenal Urbino perceived that "physical presence of God" which made him immune to the plague. "The house, shaded by the almond trees in the Los Evangelios park, seemed from the outside to be as ruined as the others in the colonial enclosure, but inside there was order in its beauty and an amazing light which seemed to come from a different age. The hallway led directly to a Sevillian patio, square and freshly painted white, with orange trees in blossom and the walls and floor paved with similar tiles. There was an imperceptibe murmur in the running water, pots of carnations in the cornices and cages of rare birds in the arcades. The strangest, in a large cage, were three crows which filled the patio with a unique scent. Several dogs chained to some part of the house suddenly began to bark, maddened by the smell of a stranger, but a woman's shout silenced them at once, and numerous cats jumped out from everywhere and hid themselves among the flowers, frightened by the authority of the voice. There followed a silence so penetrating that, through the confusion of the birds and the murmuring of the water passing over the stones, the desolate breath of the sea could be perceived".

García Márquez, Gabriel, *Love in the Time of Cholera*

More than pantheistic simplism, this conviction of the instrumental role of material as an approach to truth constitutes a moral programme which has fundamentally nourished American art, from the bitter desolation of the tales of Juan Rulfo to the ethical simplicity of the *Odes* of Pablo Neruda or the roguish tactility of the stories of Jorge Amado.

An identical desire gives life to the energetic brushstrokes of Armando Reverón (Venezuela) on rough canvases which, between lines that are almost evasive, transpose to the cloth the open images dissolved by the tropical light; the radical conceptualism of the *Bólides* by Hélio Oiticica (Brazil), boxes freed from all iconography in which the materiality denuded of sands and pigments celebrates colour without any tendentious manipulations; or to the playful apparatuses of Julio Le Parc (Argentina) under lights that make them disappear between reflections and shadows which reveal the material enfolding them and transform the tangible into the instrument of its own transposition.

Architecture is able to scrutinise and celebrate matter with technological innovations that symbolise progress, such as in the house of Amancio Williams (Argentina) in Mar del Plata, heroically raised over a gorge, or it can deliver itself up to the immanent materiality of natural situations, such as in the house by Carlos Raúl Villanueva (Venezuela) in Caraballeda and its spaces, arranged in continuity and diluted in the contrasts and nuances of a luminosity which playfully appropriates the site weaving the spaces into it. Thus, as postulate or as consubstantiation, with technical rationality or with haptic pleasure, concrete materiality is assumed as an investigation into the order of the world and for the purpose of transcending the mere evidence by transforming it into a definite experience.

More recent works emphasise this ethical sense inherent in matter. The poetic silence and precise simplicity of construction of the Gerazzi house, by Paulo Mendes da Rocha (see page 16); the didactic classifica-

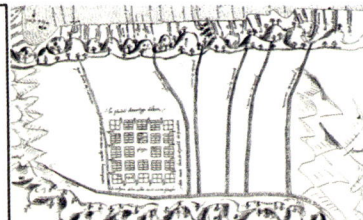

Bibliographical and professional details of the architects included in this book are on page 168.

Asturias, Miguel Ángel, *The Mirror of Lida Sal*

Fuentes, Carlos, *Terra Nostra*

tion of a strict palette of materials in the neoplasticist arrangement of the LE house, by TEN Architects (page 24); the effective contrasts of light as spatial material in the Caracola house, by Enrique Browne (page 32); the revealing confrontation between the amiable interior and the massive exterior of the Horas Claras house, by Juan Manuel Peláez (page 38); the careful dedication to detail in the construction of the Lott house, by Carlos Jiménez (page 46) from the entity of a precise materiality; the regularity given by the standardised size of the bricks, in the house in San Isidro by Billoch / Dahl-Rocha / Ramos (page 54), constructively intensifying the order, forms and articulations of the site; or the naked immediacy of the house in Cordoba by Leopoldo Laguinge (page 62), set against the vertigo-inducing horizontal of the Pampas, all investigate the promised and indispensable materiality which reveals the "chink of an impossible (…) through which to look out onto the sky".

The Building of Tradition
Perhaps because of the alienation out of which it grew, the American soul is marked by an intense need to put down roots. Furthermore, this feeling of having been orphaned has allowed it to imagine memory as an intimate adventure and build, from the vestiges of a remembrance untinged by longing, a tradition which is hybrid, free and inclusive. As the bell-gables, planted on the nakedness of the Caribbean walls reflected an improbable Flemish memory until that memory itself became reality, the tradition evoked by diffuse remembrances supported and projected a tradition born of a fertile imagination in which the similarities, although accurate, became more interwoven and less defined over a period of time. Understood and acted upon as a process rather than a product, this tradition subverted the chronological with the divergent logic of the many processes which it drew together to nourish what was coming into being with an intuitive recognition of what could have been. Thus, to remember is to intervene in time and to imagine it from the standpoint of the adventure of constructing, in much the same way as Friar Julián demanded of the Court Chronicler: "Why do you only tell us that which we already know, rather than reveal to us that of which we are still in ignorance? Why do you only describe to us this time and this space, rather than all of those invisible times and spaces which ours contain? Why, in short, are you content with the pathetic dripping of the mere succession of events, when your pen offers you the plenitude of a universe of simultaneous occurrences?"

Inhabiting time as an inclusive and dynamic territory, the American spirit builds its tradition by blending memories which describe the future. From the telluric baroque of José Lezama Lima's *Paradise* to the all-enveloping fugues of Heitor Villalobos' *Bachianas* or the historic sagas of Augusto Roa Bastos, the ineluctable need to explain and place the juxtaposed presences has been a recurring theme in American art. They enrich the syncretic landscapes of Wilfredo Lam (Cuba), with their manifold crosses of black magic rituals, Afro-Caribbean imagery and present-day aesthetics, the playful installations of Charo Oquet (Dominican Republic) as popular ceremonies which integrate personal history, animism and kitsch, or the disturbing photographs of Luis González Palma (Guatemala) in which everyday objects and faces in the street welcome and project their penetrating expressions and the bleakness with which they look at each other, the multi-directional mystery of a sought-after memory.

The simplicity of popular architecture offers itself with evocative transparency to unravel the codes in this process of building a liberating tradition. It was in this context that the houses which Sergio Larraín (Chile) built for himself and his daughter on the foundations of a modest existing construction appropriated the latter's colloquial simplicity and reformulated it in clearly modern grammar. And the paradigmatic house by Luis Barragán (México) in Tacubaya also deliberately articulates walls, lights and colours in a sensual intrigue which transmigrates memories onto insinuating presences, as surprising as they are recognisable. By invoking the built past or summoning the forces which build the present, as text or as the context of a tradition which embraces without entrapping, American architecture absorbs and rejects with identical vehemence the mysteries of its history.

The building of tradition continues to constitute a fundamental American programme. The search for the site in its constructive tradition in the Floridia house, by María de la Guardia and Teófilo Victoria (page 68); the clear material and formal situations which metaphorically historicise the territory of the house by Mariano Clusellas in Colonia del Sacramento (page 74); the Caribbean codes of the exultant modernity of the House on the Lake, by Carlos Betancourt (page 82); the typological echoes which sustain the continuous spatiality of the house in Lomas de la Lagunita by Larrañaga / Obadía (page 90); the archetypal recurrence throughout the successive patios of the La Queja house, by Benjamín Barney-Caldas (page 98); the ancestral simplicity of the Casabe house, by Ana Loreto (page 104), serenely integrated into and given over to the natural splendour; or the insinuating re-conception of the primitive hut in the raw and elemental simplicity of the D'Alessandro house, by Andrade / Morettin (page 110)—all combine to invoke a tradition which evokes life from a time which "trembles, dilates and bursts, discovering unforeseen forms, dazzling spaces without a trace of anything which might have preceded us."

The Formation of Territory

While some cultures conceive architecture as a means of protection against natural hazards, American buildings manage to form a harmonious and complete territory by modulating the inhabited space as an integrated, permeable, multiple and continuous whole of physical locations. Like the cattle ranches which formed the landscape of Paraguaná by contrasting their serene inner order with the crude vastness of the desert, the signs of the visible territory depart dialectically from the forces and impulses of a territory of the senses to allow life and the spaces which house it to flow and interchange with transparent ease. The world which remains in hope of its own possibility becomes a certainty provided that the territory which is built realises the myths, landmarks and rituals of an order which, by making itself felt, begins to reveal itself, in continuous dialogue, intensely and even agonisingly, with the diffuse promise of a world full of stimulating signs, such as when "Doctor Montsalvatje, holding high his head next to the stake, pointed to the distant meseta, bathed in deep blue towards which the moon was rising: 'Nobody knows what lies behind those Shapes', he said, in a tone reminiscent of childhood emotion. We all wanted to stand up, to set off walking, to arrive before dawn at the gate of wonders. Once more the waters of the Parima lagoon will shine. Once more the citadels of Manoa will be raised within us. The possibility of their existence was once

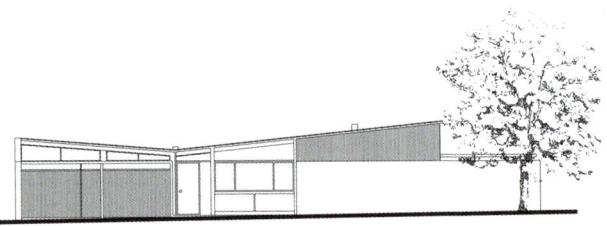

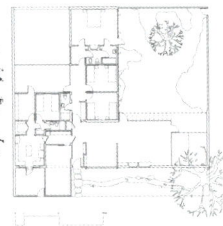

Garmendia, Salvador, *Memories of Altagracia*

Carpentier, Alejo, *The Lost Steps*

again suggested, because their myth lived on in the imagination of all of those who dwelt in the vicinity of the Jungle, in other words, of the Unknown."

This desire to read territory as a form of promise constitutes another basic theme of American art, present in the tenacious interweaving of the sagas of Rómulo Gallegos with the spaces in which they take place, the multiple references in "salsa" as a compilation of diverse testimonies, or the precise network of places, events and characters in the stories of Mario Vargas Llosa. This desire is also present in the interior landscapes of Roberto Matta (Chile), with the constructive familiarity of infinite atmospheres which float imposingly close, the sheltered places between the stones and wood sculpted by Gonzalo Fonseca (Uruguay), enclaves of a possible world on a support converted into a world by the force of those signs, or the organically geometric fabric of the *Reticuláreas* by Gego (Gertrudis Goldschmidt, Venezuela) which, with steely fragility, enables us to see and inhabit the universe in the rhythms of its constant movement.

The clement-climate was not the only factor affecting the architecture in the area. Rather more than this was the desire to think of the world as complementary and, acting on this principle with determination, to create a territory that would suggest the area's characteristic diversity. The house by Oscar Niemeyer (Brazil) in Canoas is anchored to the site by a rock which, as an architectural piece, interlaces house and landscape in a continuum of fluid spaces and enfolding curves; on the other hand, the access loggia of the house by Mario Payssé Reyes (Uruguay) in Carrasco, joins building and site using a space which is simultaneously—almost ambiguously—internal and external and which plays down those complementary values with the expansive intimacy of an effervescent vision and the reality of its concrete tactility. With the visible signs of a friendly natural environment or the sensitive constructions of a dearly loved landscape, the American territory, by intensifying its many nuances, brings together harmoniously its seemingly inhabitable sites.

This attempt to fashion the American territory as symbol of its possible spaces continues in more recent examples. The minimal tectonics of the house on the banks of the Paraná by Rafael Iglesia (page 118), judiciously measuring the depth of the Pampas; the notation of the site through the didactic order of forms and materials in Renato Anelli's house at the Paulinia dam (page 126); the inclusion of the mountain range to delimit the domestic precincts of the Posada house by Echeverri Architects (page 132); the multi-faceted interior territory of the Amsterdam house by Teodoro González de León (page 138) as a collection of evocative signs; the fluid spatial alternations of La Ribereña by Jimmy Alcock (page 146) which interchange territorial categories in order to integrate them into a total experience; the light structural intrigue of the La Reina house by Cristian Boza (page 154), which modulates a well-ordered landscape; and the dynamic interweaving of the Negro house, by Kalach and Álvarez (page 160), with the wooded slope to which it gives structure and in which the house seems to search for completeness—all these give form to a territory in which values and forces may nourish themselves intermingling to learn "a elocuaçào horizontal de seu verso;/ a geúrgica de cordel, ininterrupta,/ narrada em voz e siléncio paralelos".

Cabral de Nelo Meto, Joao, *O mar e o canavial*

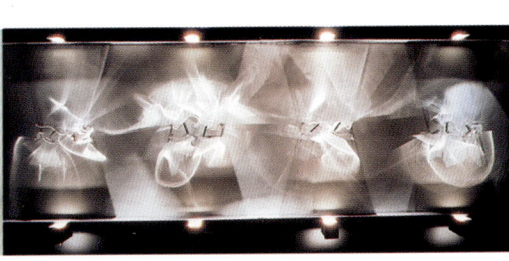

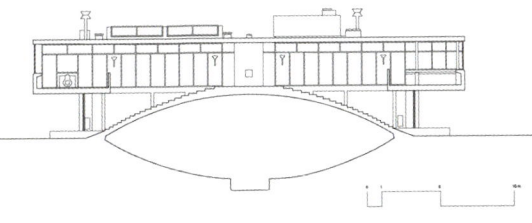

Autobiographies of a Place 11

Pérez Oramas, Luis, *Duchamp y la fábula jurásica*

Coda: Self-portrait with Open Book
(…) to show that the visual part of an art of the vision is not limited to that which can be seen within the borders of the image.

Luis Pérez Oramas

Searching for life among memories and desires, things and possibilities, matter and presences, the unfinished journey towards the realisation of the American Utopia continues to explore the tense harmony between notions and actions. The gates of this riddle are many and entwined and its mysteries may prove to be as deceiving for the unguarded soul as the song of a false siren. Passing through these gates is to assume the risk of deceptive enchantment with the thoughtful abandon of one who knows that only by losing oneself can one find oneself and that knowing requires seeing beyond that which is looked at.

If Utopia makes the possible indispensable, even while knowing it can never be attained but is seen as a challenge which finds in the awareness of its impossibility renewed motives for making it real, the *raison* of the American soul is to investigate this improbable possibility in order to transform the experience of the concrete into an exploration of the intangible: to experience things from the evidences of a materiality which only reveals itself in its immanence; to penetrate time as an adventurer who invokes memory for the sole purpose of learning to imagine; to inhabit the visible as unfathomable traces of a sensitivity made anxious for awareness. This being while in the act of being, from that which we have been and towards that which we wish to be, means being with the world defined from the perspective of a desire to transcend it, by removing piece by piece that which separates us from the truth.

Baccino Ponce de León, Napoleón, *Maluco*

There can be no doubt that the journey is not yet, and never will be, over. And this certainty is surely what lures us on, because "(…) for the true navigator there is no other destination than the infinite solitude of the oceans and the maddening aroma of impossible islands. (…) because you, and I, and all of us, are not unlike pilgrims lost in the desert, and our dreams are mirages. Mirages which intensify our thirst without quenching it. For it is our very thirst which tells us we are still alive."

1   Coastline of the Paria Peninsula
2   River Bamba, 16th century print
3   Plan of the city of Caracas made by the Governor Juan de Pimentel in 1578, eleven years after the founding of the city
4   Patio house
5   Doorway from the presbytery to the sacristy, Trinity Mission House, Paraguay
6   Ocotlán Sanctuary, Tlaxcala, Mexico
7   Church of the Rosary, Ouro Preto, Brazil
8   Torre-Tagle Palace, Lima, Peru
9   House in La Otra Banda, Dominican Republic
10   Side doorway of the Cathedral, Puno, Peru
11   House in Guanare, decorated windows
12   House on a country estate, passageway
13   Rufino Tamayo, *Two figures in blue*, oil on cloth, 1961
14   Lina Bo Bardi, house of glass, exterior view
15   Emilio Duhart, Duhart house, made façade and floor plan
16   Luis Barragán. Studio-House Luis Barragán, Tacubaya, México, 1947
17   House in Angostura, exterior view
18   Armando Reveron, *Light behind my bower*, oil on cloth, 1926
19   Helio Oticica, *Box bolide 12, archeologic*, acrylic paint with sand on wooden structure, nylon mesh, corrugated cardboard, mirror, glass, stones, sand and installation with fluorescent bulb, 1964-65.
20   Julio le Parc, *Mural of continuous light*, 1966
21   Amancio Williams, house in Mar del Plata, section, 1950
22   Carlos Raúl Villanueva, Sotavento house, view towards the interior, 1952
23   House of the Iron Windows, corner detail
24   Wifredo Lam, *Light of clay*, oil on cloth, 1950, Museum of Fine Arts Collection, Caracas
25   Charo Oquet, *Flowers for Doña Josefa Mota de Flores*, installation, 2000
26   Luis González Palma, *Recycling*, impression in hand-painted silver gelatine, embroidered brocade, Kodalith, 76 ×155 cm, 2000
27   Sergio Larraín, house of the architect and house of Barbara Larrain, floor plan, 1962
28   La Sirena cattle ranch, exterior view
29   Roberto Matta, *Open Earth*, oil on cloth, 1957
30   Gonzalo Fonseca, *False Pendulum*, marble sculpture
31   Gego, *Reticulárea*, 1969.
32   Oscar Niemeyer, house in Canoas, floor plan, 1952
33   Mario Payssé Reyes, house in Carrasco, interior view, 1953
34   Carlos Raúl Villanueva, Caoma house, view of the garden from the living room, 1952
35   Ana Mendieta, *Silhouette in Iowa*, 1995

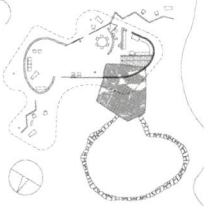

21 houses at the start of the 21st century

Gerazzi House

Sao Paulo, Brazil
1989-1991

Paulo Mendes da Rocha

Collaborators: *Alexandre Delijaicv, Geni Takeuchi Sugai, Pedro Mendes da Rocha*
Assistant: *María Luisa Becheroni*
Structure and foundations: *CONSCAL-Consultas y Cálculos LTDA*
Engineer in charge: *Siguer Mitsutani*
Hydraulics and electricity: *APF Engenharia s/c LTDA*
Engineers in charge: *Antônio Alexandre Pupo Filho, Antônio Gerassi Neto*
Builder: *Reago Indústria e Comércio S/A*
Constructor: *José Thomaz*
Floors: *Ladrilar Indústria e Comércio LTDA*
Windows: *Metalúrgica Garra LTDA*
Kitchen: *Kitchens Comércio de Aparelhos Domésticos*
Photography: *Cynthia Yendo*

1 Sketch
2 Upper floor
3 Longitudinal section

Opposite page: Detail of the access level from the rear patio

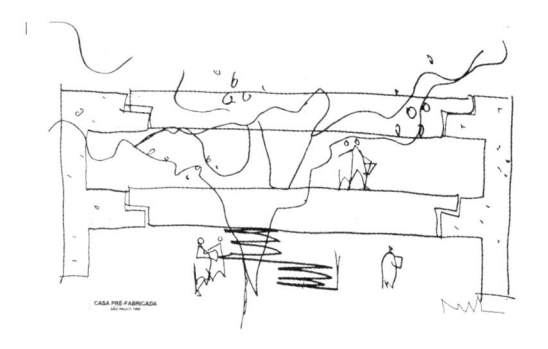

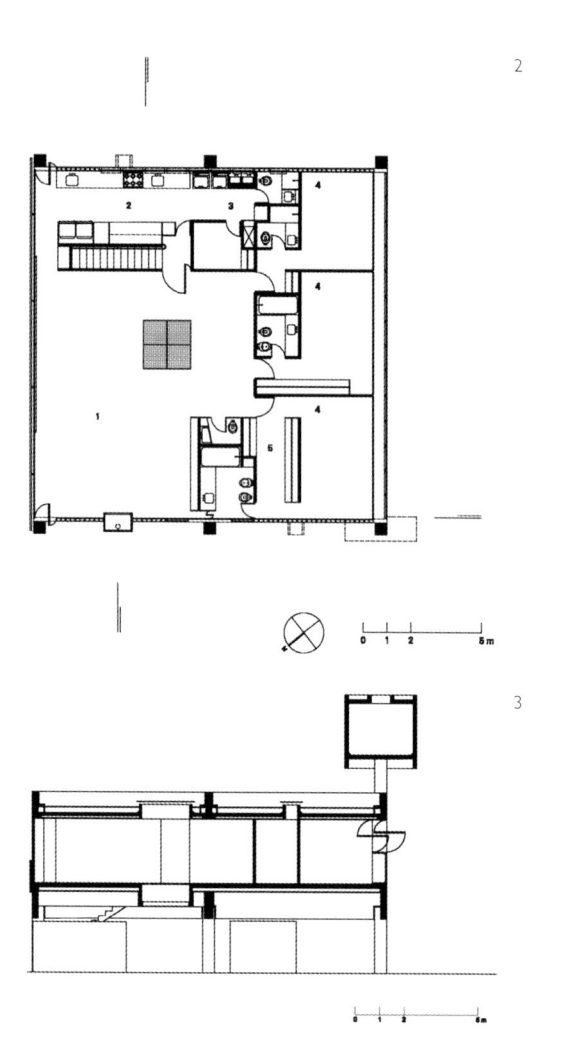

The intelligent use of prefabricated systems of reinforced and prestressed concrete, produced by local industry and adopted as a technological heritage which challenges the creativity of the architect, underpins a form of architecture that achieves the revealing encounter between formal invention and building techniques. Six perimeter columns support two planes of concrete which frame the habitable space like a continuous platform floating among the treetops. The elevation of this structure enables total continuity of the terrain, from the street to the recreation area at the rear of the site, where the swimming pool nestles beneath the box-like living quarters. Only a service block and the arrangement of plain but intensely worked stairs, give some degree of privacy to this space and establish a relative sense of direction. For the rest, the roof barely modulates the space to show the fragile intimacy of domestic activity.

On the upper level, the partitions establish functional strata which with efficient simplicity classify the activities of the house. A skylight aligned to a grid in the floor permits the social area to be separated into three continuous but identifiable territories (living room, dining room and rest area), while, as if evoking a patio, it establishes the only vertical connection between the planes of the house and between the house itself, the ground and the sky. The floors of patterned tiles extend the continuity of space outwards with a pattern which is also industrial but somewhat more festive. The horizontal character of the windows, clearly related to the modern utopia of universal space, emphasises the abstraction which gives preference to the ethical pleasure of the physical evidence over the accidental nature of the pleasing formal production.

A pleasure compounded, as the architect testified, by the high level of efficiency in the organisation and co-ordination of all phases of construction and in the optimisation of the budget.

Gerazzi House 17

1 Living room, details of cross ventilation
2 General view of the sitting area in the main living room

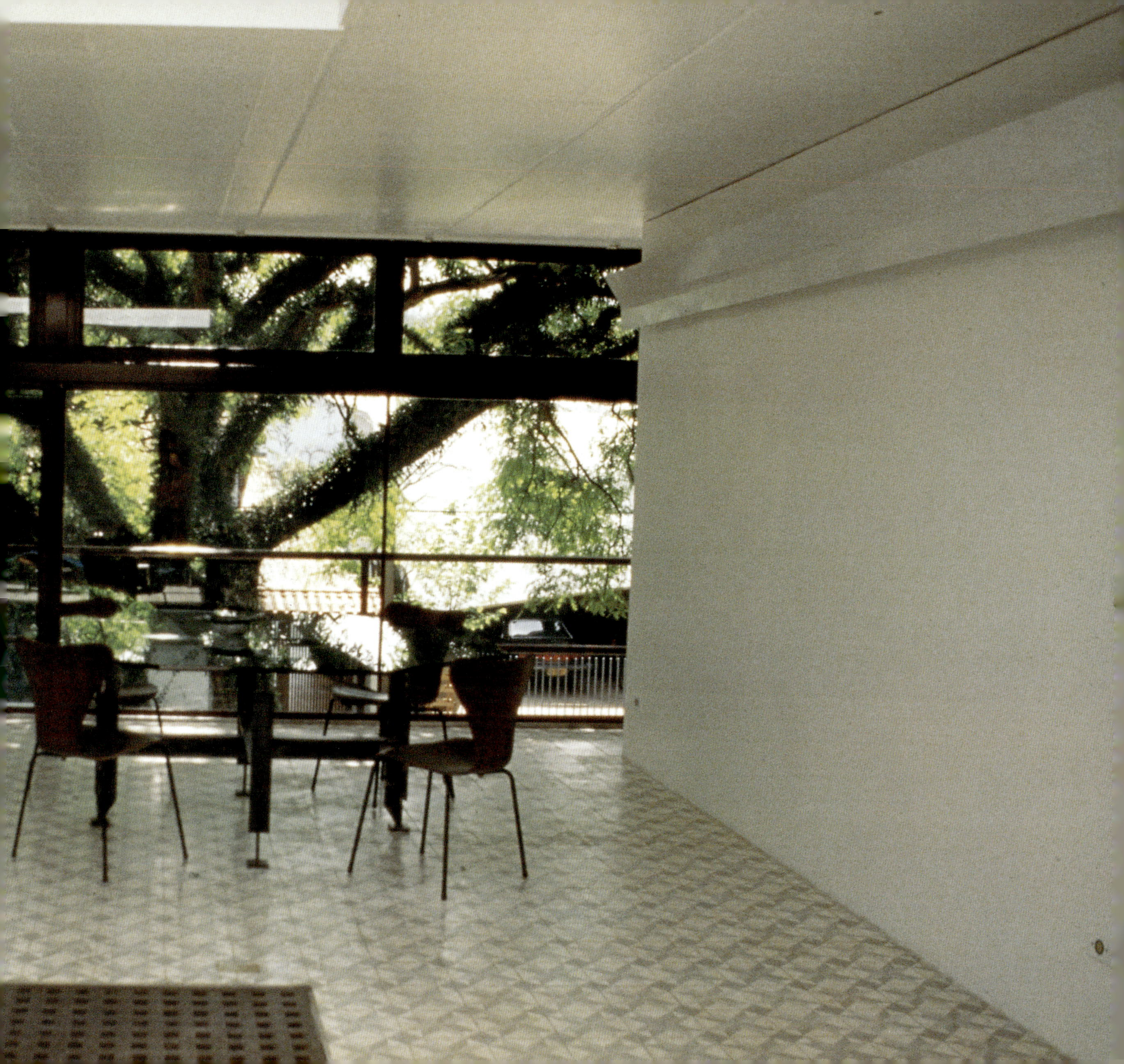

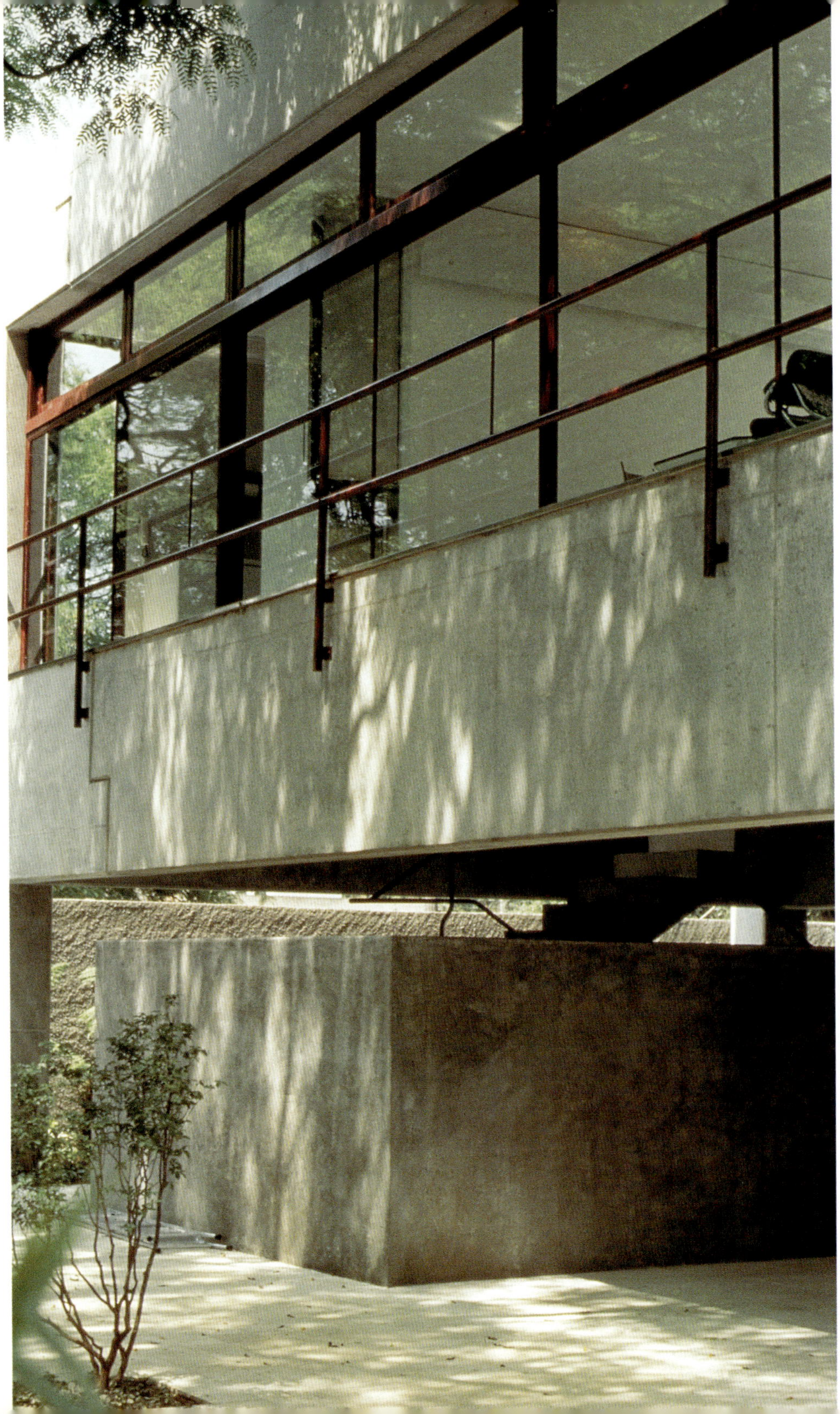

1 Detail of the main façade and the access stairs
2 Living room. Private area with detail of skylight and metal grid for light and ventilation

1 Section. Construction detail
2 Detail of volumes of the access stairs and the support structure in the sleeping area
Opposite page: Detail of the stairs

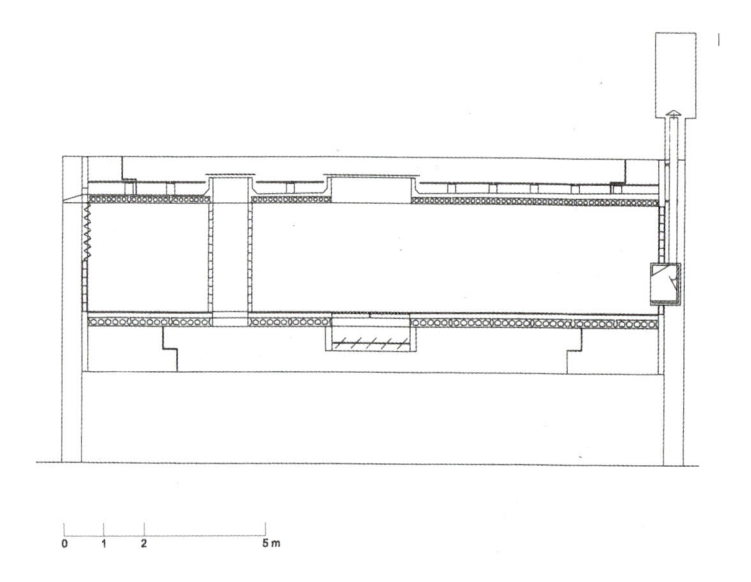

22

Gerazzi House

LE House

Colonia Condesa, Mexico City, Mexico
1994-1995

TEN Architects
Enrique Norten /
Bernardo Gómez-Pimienta

Project team: *Carlos Ordoñez, Gustavo Espitia*
Model: *Gustavo Espitia, Jaime Cabezas*
Structural engineer: *Colinas de Buen Ingenieros S.A.*
Installations: *Tecnoproyectos S.A.*
General contractor: *Grupo Baia S.A.*
Photography: *Luis Gordoa, Timothy Hursley*

On a 170 sq.m site, in a densely populated residential area of Mexico City, the LE House shares adjoining walls and a continuous façade with its neighbours. It offers a clear contrast, along the longitudinal axis of the terrain, between a compactly built mass which occupies approximately half of the area and a mass of air which, from the other half, provides the ventilation, lighting and privacy of the rooms.

On the lower level, which functions as a kind of penetrable basement, are the garage and the service areas. The second level, as a traditional *piano nobile*, comprises the principal spaces of the house, opening directly onto the patio on the roof of the service areas forming a recreation area. A flight of stairs at the rear, leading onto a secondary patio, provides access to the bedrooms on the upper storey, and to the study-library below.

The layout organises parallel strata which define the functional areas of the house and interrelate them with gradual permeability. The northern boundary is defined by a narrow block of deposits. Parallel to this runs the corridor, along which are the living spaces, opening to the patio via a glass plane. A screen of wooden strips, like a sun protection plane, gives spatial depth to both the interior and the exterior and forms the façade of the house over the patio, flat like the façade over the street but, unlike the latter, transparent and permeable. Between this plane and beneath a cantilever, the bedrooms lead onto a fragile balcony which provides an alternative connection between them. Transversely, the internal spaces relate to the spatial modulations of the patio and are interlaced with it through the continuity of surfaces and materials.

View of the interior from the patio

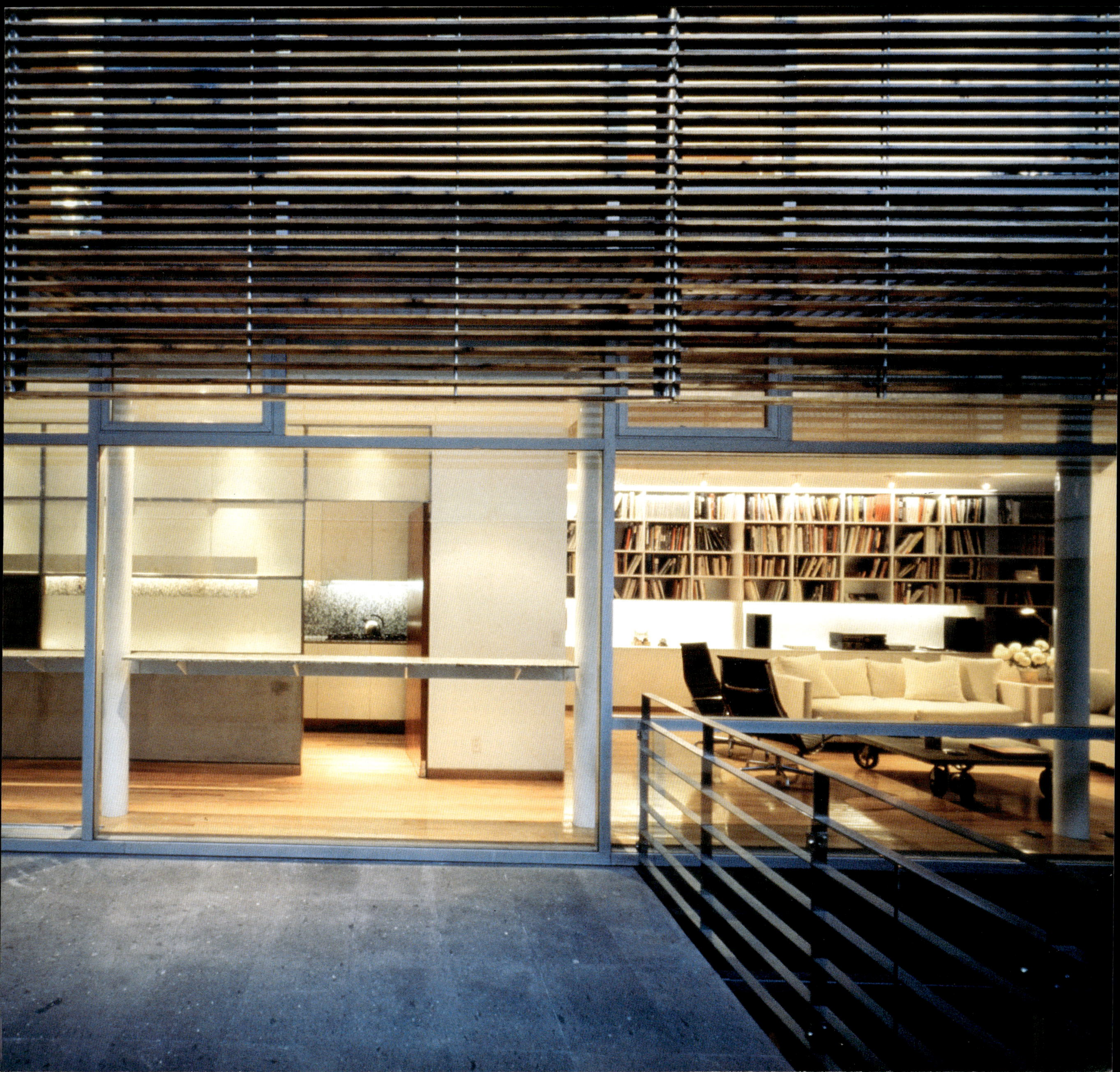

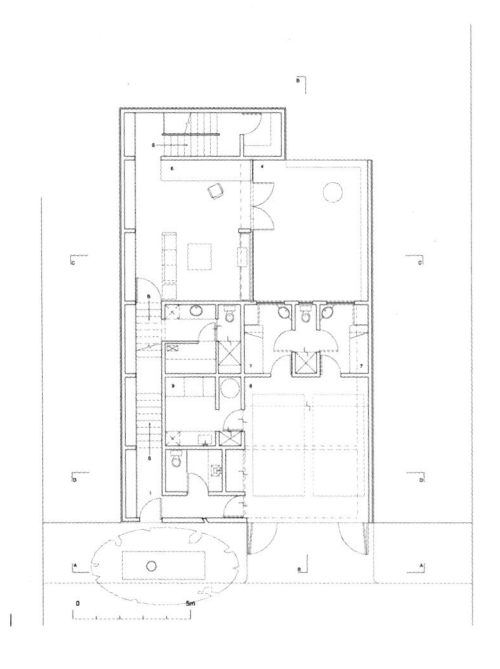

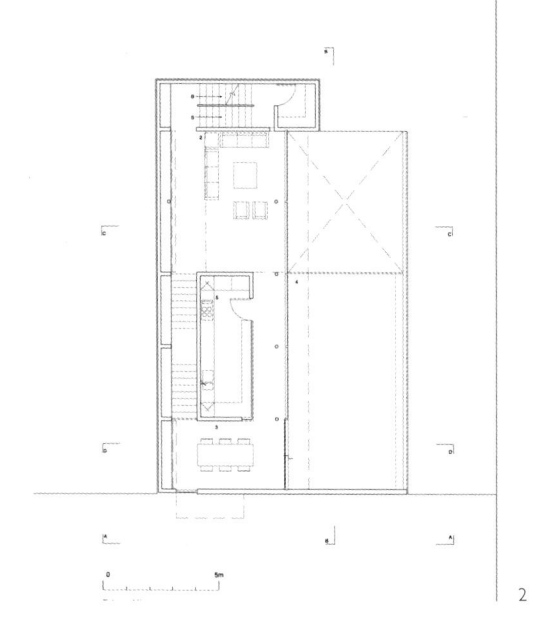

1 Floor plan of the access level
2 Floor plan of the first level
3 Floor plan of the second level
4 Roof plan
Opposite page: View of the living room

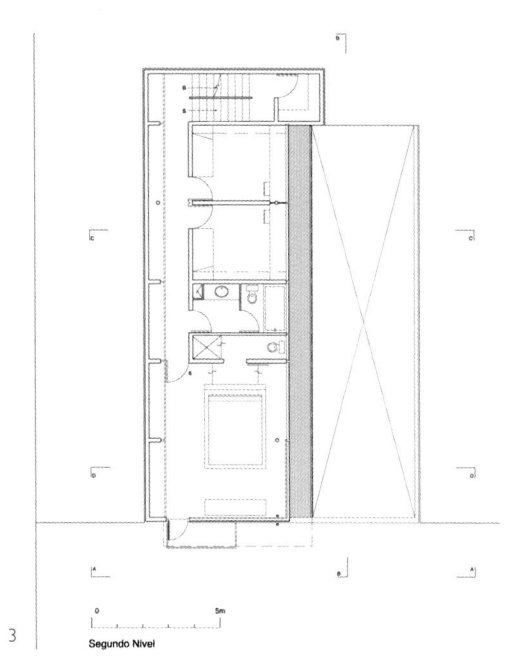

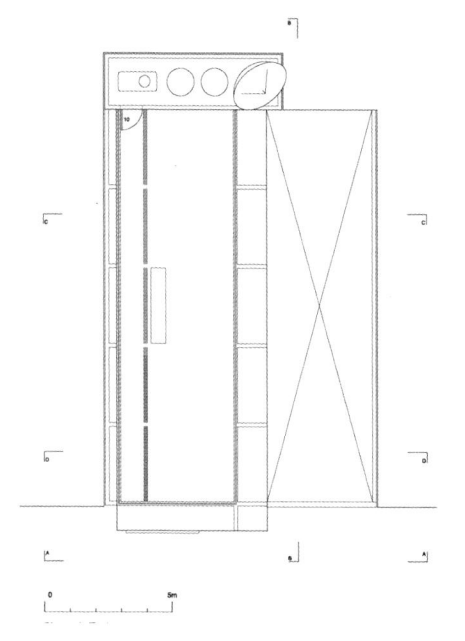

Segundo Nivel

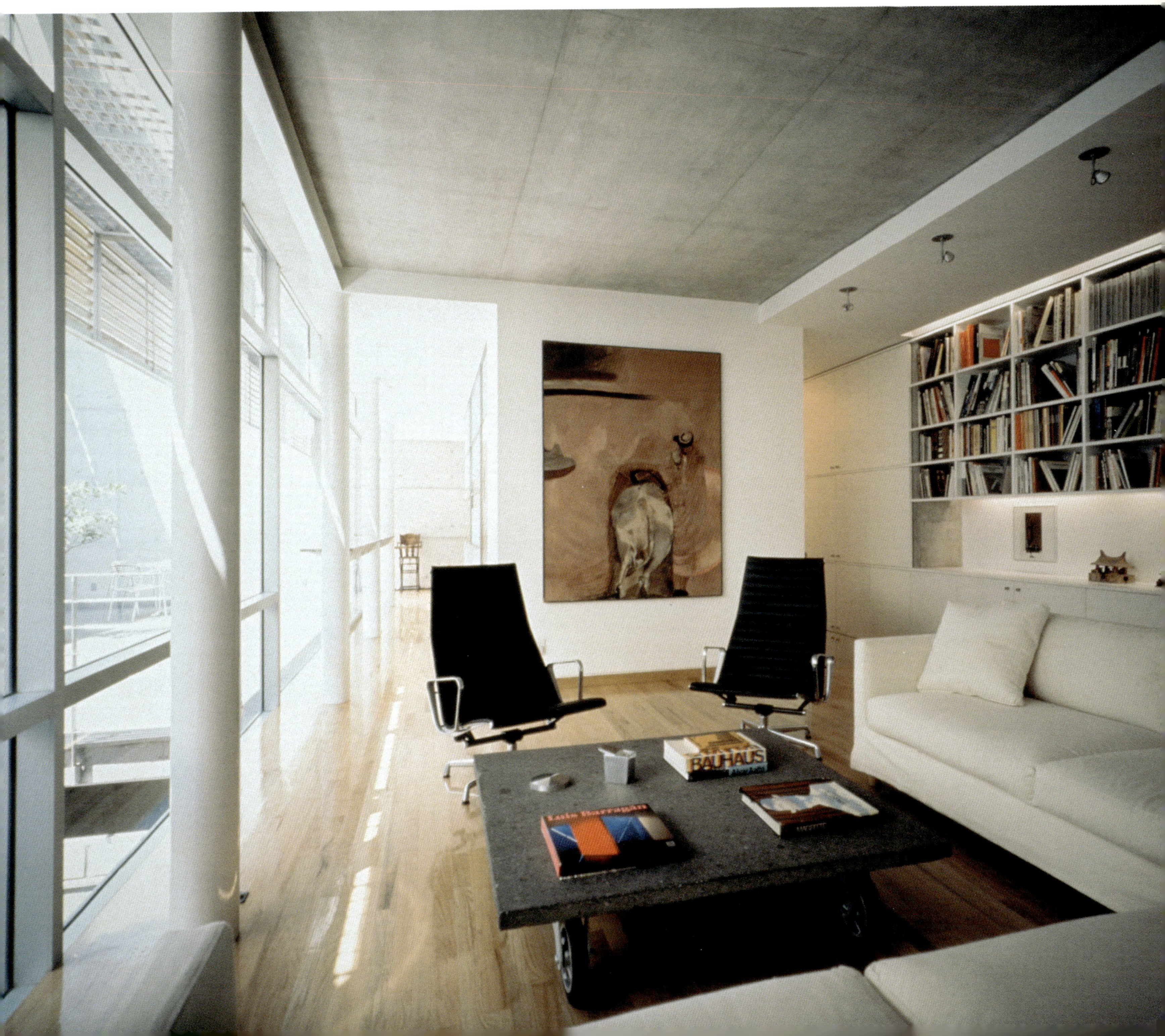
BAUHAUS
Luis Barragan

1

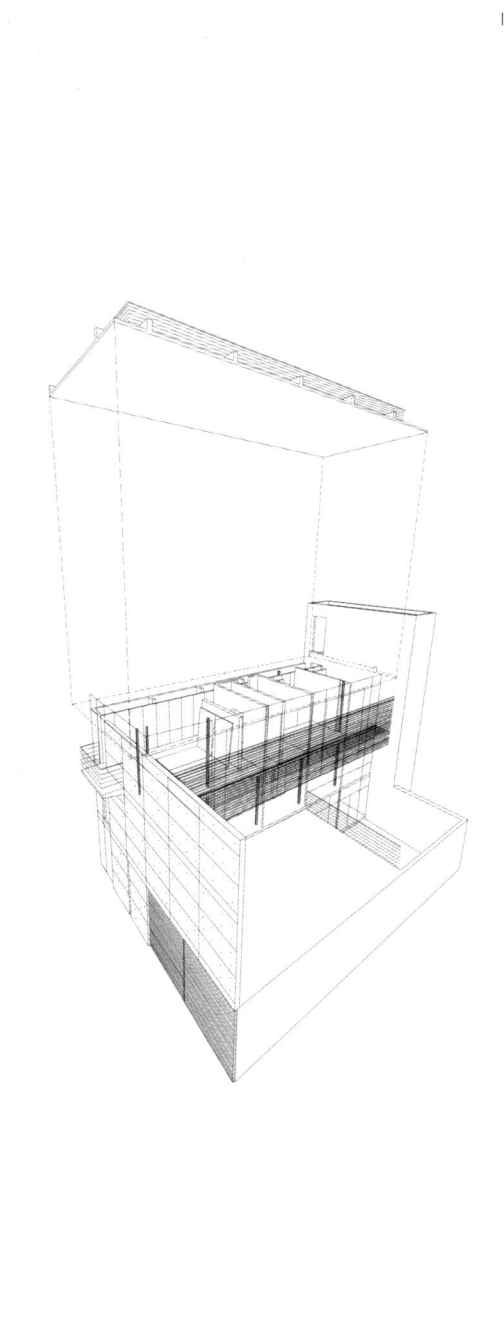

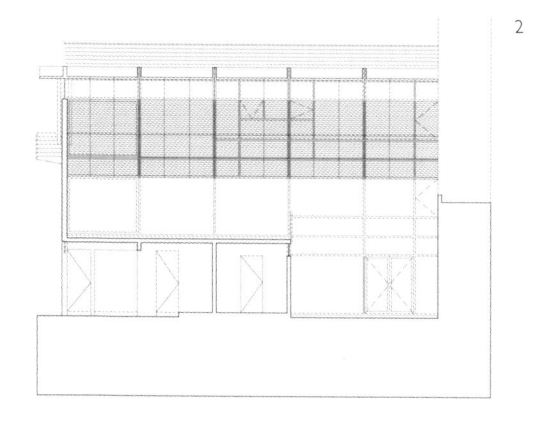

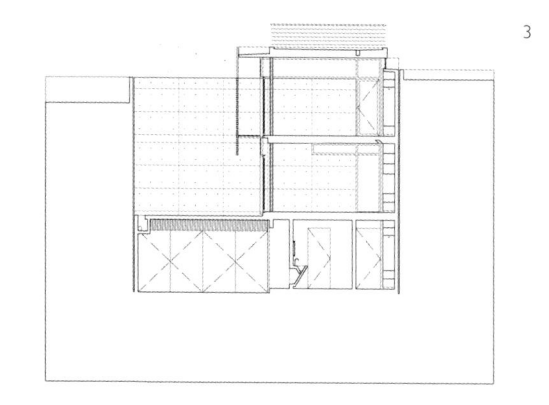

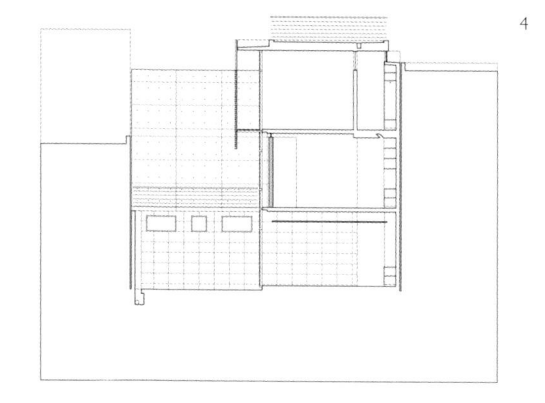

2

3

4

28

1 Axonometric projection
2 Longitudinal section
3 Cross section of dining room and terrace
4 Cross section of living room and indoor patio
5 Interior detail of column
6 Passageway

1 View of the dining room
2 Outside passage between windows and wooden lattice

2

Caracola House
Santiago de Chile, Chile
1985-1987

Enrique Browne

Collaborators: *Jorge Campos / Ricardo Cruz*
Photography: *Roberto de la Fuente*

1 Sketch
2 View towards corridor and dining room

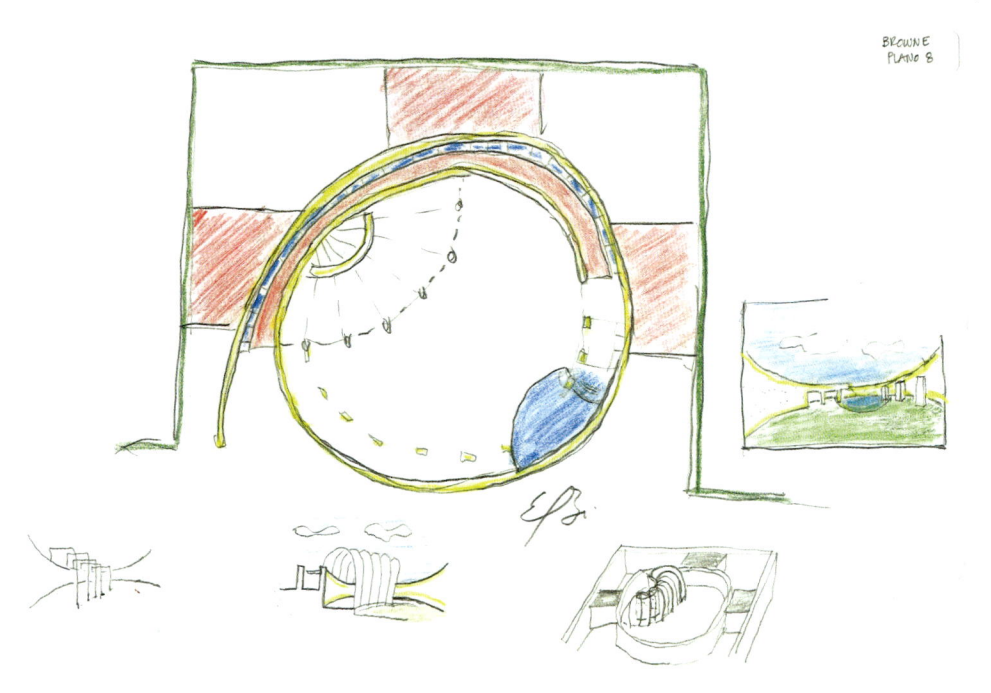

Light is the main feature of this house and the resource around which its spatial sequences are arranged. The square-shaped site is almost totally occupied by a large oval form at its centre, following the main diagonal towards the north, and a group of spaces arranged between this interior figure and the boundaries. Thus, the experience of the house takes place within the spiral which, though surrounding the oval, seeks the centre, as if winding itself around it, and which, once it has reached that centre, expands again outwards towards the garden and the swimming pool—also defined from the starting point of the dominant figure.

The difference of 1.2 m between the ground level of the site and the street is used to give a hierarchical structure to the main areas and contiguity of the sequence with a gradual descent which ritualises the spatial process around the main space. The private areas, arranged peripherally and at street level, are broken up to form small patios which identify their own place and hierarchy. The arrangement of the common areas defines the shape of the oval patio. The spiral wall which influences the direction of movement, and classifies the uses of the house, is accompanied by a linear skylight which establishes the horizontal datum of the house and bathes the corridor with its intense white light. At the end of the wall, a water chute seems almost to pour the wall out over the swimming pool in the patio, as if pouring the force of the light over the movement of the water and the expanse of the air.

Coloured panes of glass are used to reflect light from above onto the white walls. Thus, the dining room—the symbolic nucleus of the house—acquires the golden tone of its skylights, while the gallery maintains a white clarity and the covered terrace is illuminated in deep blue through an opening in the roof.

2

1

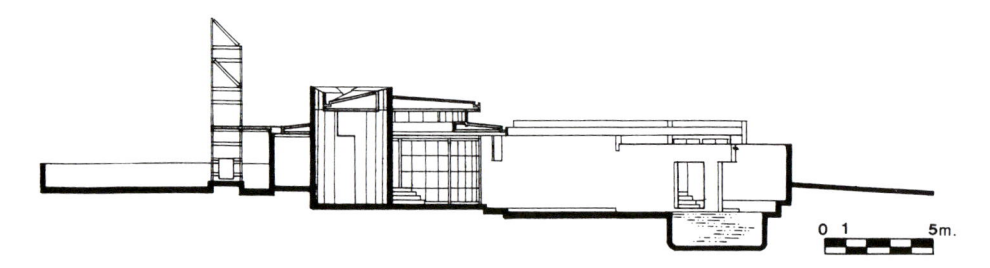

2

1 Section
2 View from the interior patio at night
3 Geometric design
4 Dining room
5 Floor plan

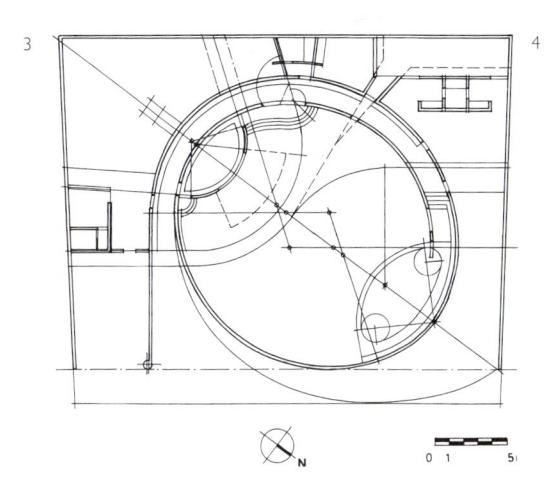

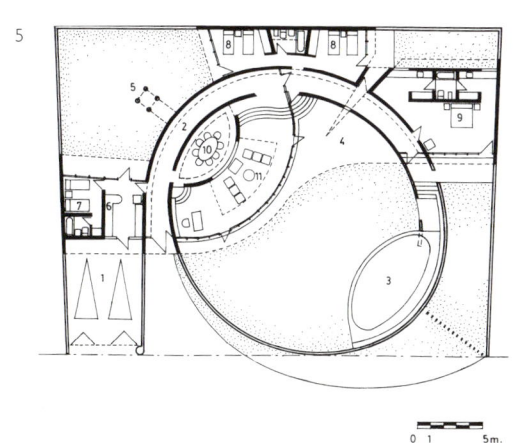

Caracola House 35

1   Water chute
2   Sketch
Opposite page: View towards the garden

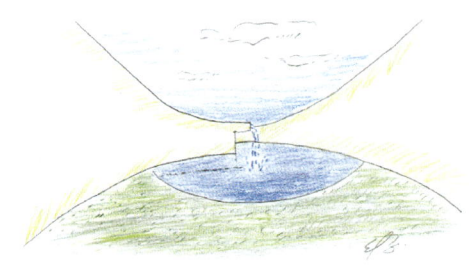

Caracola House 37

Horas Claras House

El Retiro, Antioquia, Colombia
1997-1998

Juan Manuel Peláez

Colour consultants: *Alberto Sierra / Luis Fernando Peláez*
Foundations design: *Engineer Luis Bernardo González*
Geologic survey: *Engineer Librado Gallego*
Builder: *Juan Manuel Peláez Freidel*
Photography: *Juan Manuel Peláez Freidel*

Rising like bastions over the voluptuous topography of El Retiro, a mountain village 30 km from Medellín, are two towers linked by a terrace. They almost seem to be just another part of the rugged and uneven landscape. The way in which the towers are arranged around the terrace emphasises the way the composition opens out towards the geography of the site, while the central nature of the terrace creates a focal point, a point of reference which evokes the all-embracing power of the traditional patio.

From the access level the rooms are entered from the common level which houses the living room, the dining room and the kitchen, points where the family gather together—different areas connected by a terrace. These areas can be opened out onto the terrace to form a single larger space for special occasions or during the summer while returning to the smaller, albeit fluid, scale for daily use. The bedrooms and study areas are located on independent levels in order to guarantee their privacy and create a more compartmentalised spatial density.

The outer surfaces, of concrete blocks, open more towards the north and east to gain the best views and catch the warmth of the morning sun through glass planes; they are more opaque towards the south and the west, to protect against the sun and preserve intimacy. The treatment of the floors in the approach to the house, articulated by a system of containing walls and lines of water, modulates the progressive transformation of the natural condition into architectural presence. The plainness of the architectural elements shows without affectation the purity of the materials used, to incorporate them into the serene celebration of the site through the precise use of the forms as an instrument of revelation.

1 Site plan
2 Sketch

Opposite page: View of the outside of the building

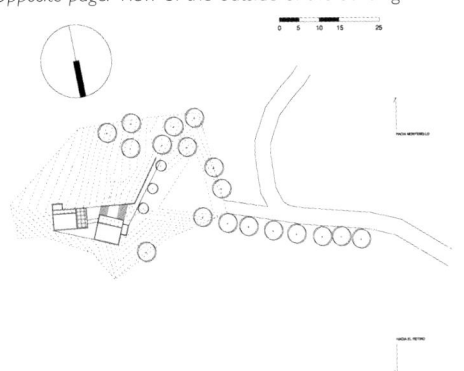

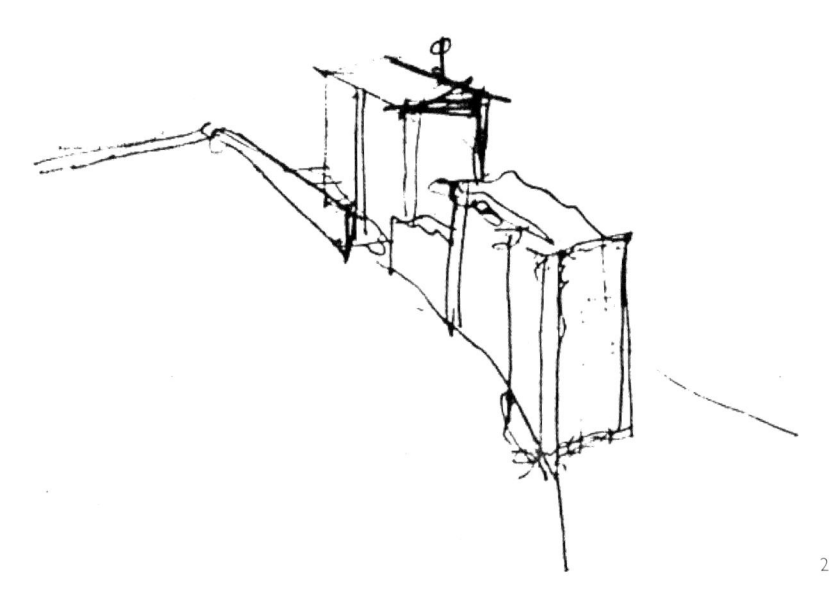

Horas Claras House 39

1 Floor level -2
2 Floor level -1
3 Floor level 0.0
4 Floor level +1
5 Floor level +2
6 Axonometric projection
7 Terrace between the two sections

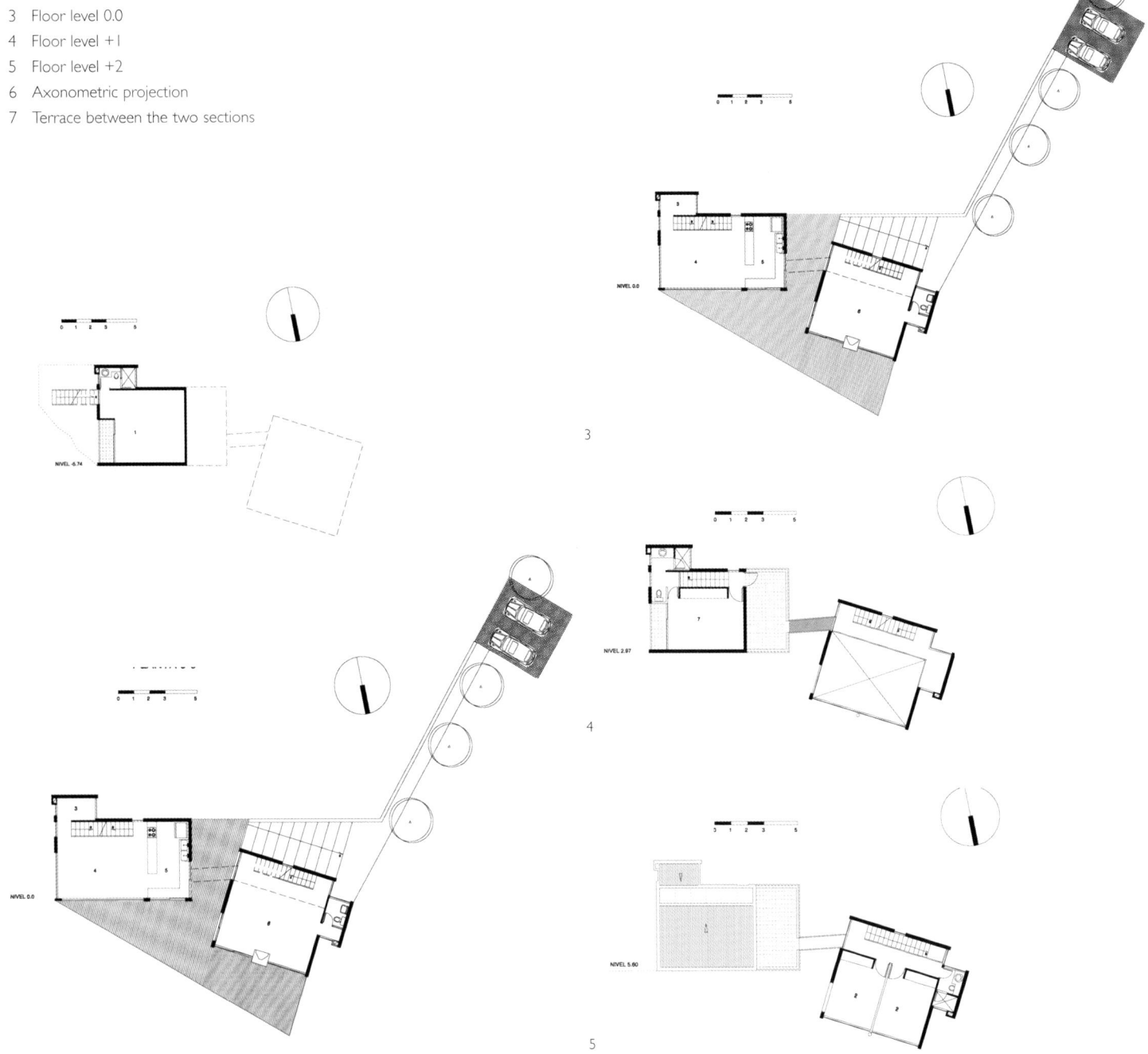

6

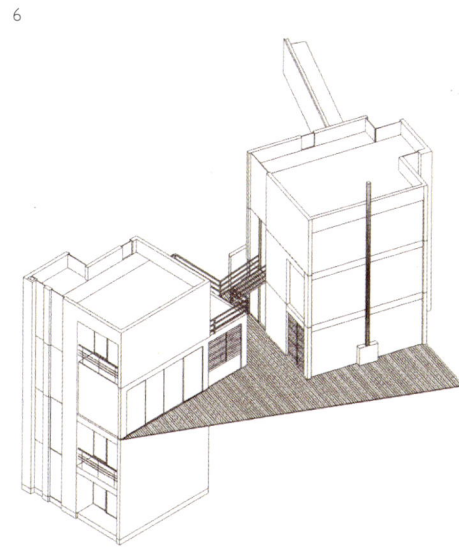

7

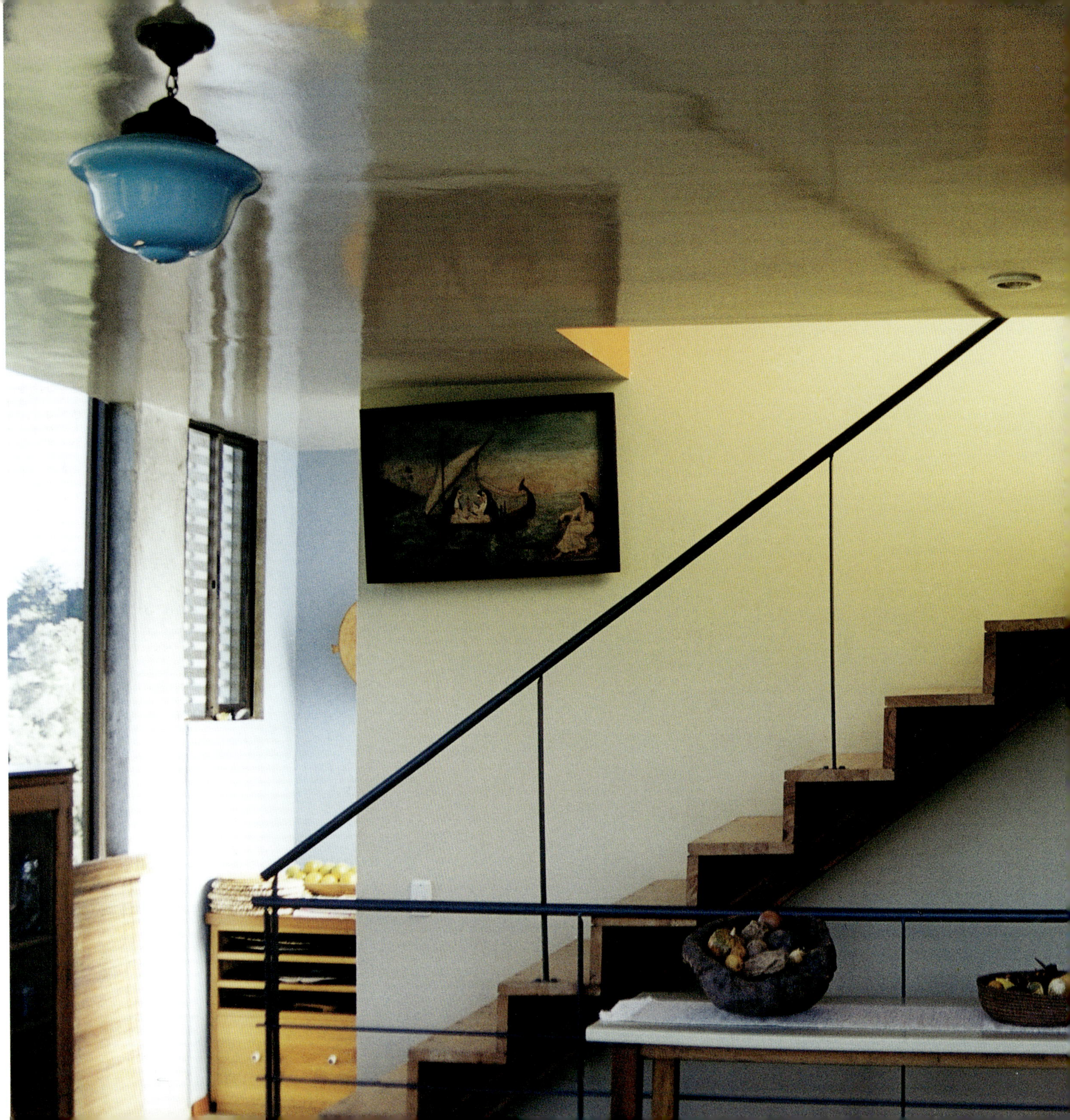

Large photo: View of the interior of the building
1 Longitudinal section
2 East face of the building
3 South face of the building

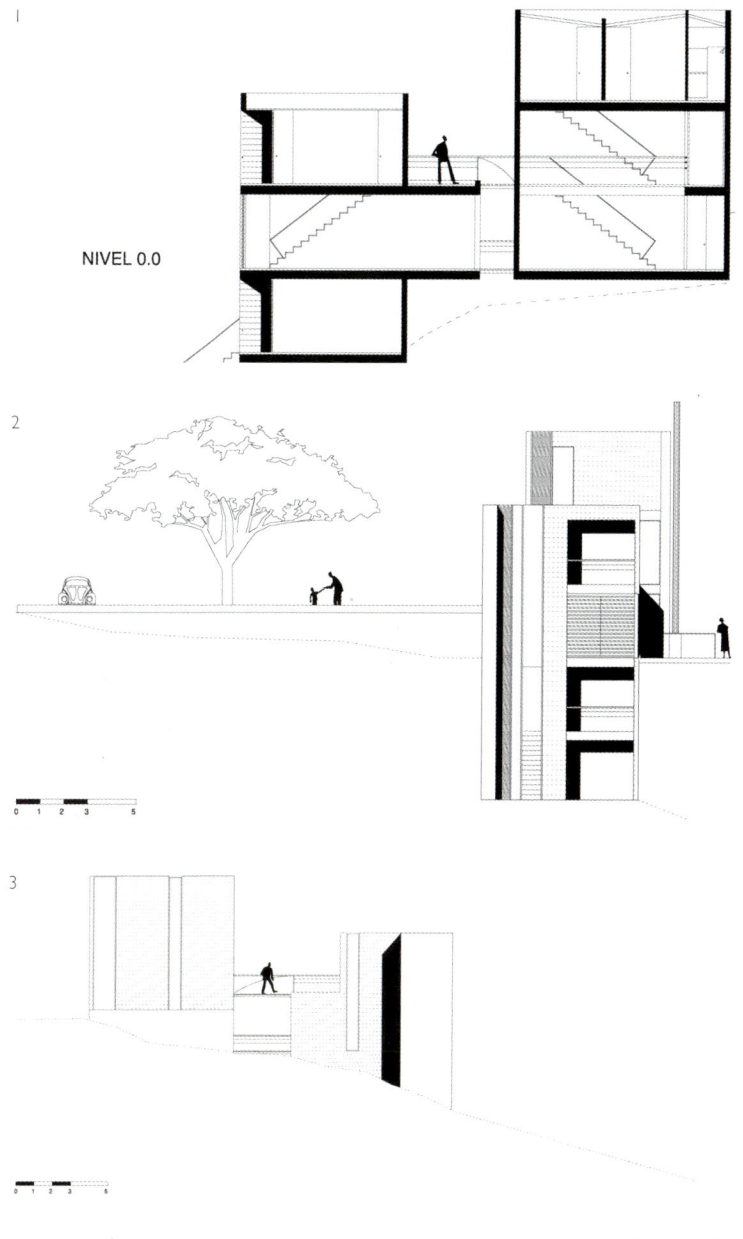

1

NIVEL 0.0

2

3

Horas Claras House 43

44

3

1 Interior view of the living room
2 Detail of the access steps
3 View of the landscape seen from the living room

Lott House
Houston, Texas, United States
1992-1994

Carlos Jiménez

Client: *Marley Scott*
Project: *Carlos Jiménez / Robert Fowler / Mason Wickman / Eric Batte / Gerard Chung*
Structures engineer: *Structural Consulting Company, Inc., Houston*
Builder: *Ted Anderson, Anderson Builders, Houston*
Photography: *Paul Hester, Hester+Hadaway Photographers, Fayetteville, Texas*

In one of the more memorable streets in the city of Houston stands the Lott House. This 400 sq.metre building in a traditional neighbourhood overlooks a street lined with mature oak trees which give the area the grandiose appearance of a covered boulevard. At the rear of the site was built an independent guest house which, it was thought, would act as a counterweight to the main building which occupies as much of the front of the site as is permitted by the regulations in force. The guest house, a third of the size of the main house, forms a backdrop parallel to the first storey, thus creating a garden in between which is open but framed by the two buildings. A high wooden fence completes this intermediary space which links both houses and forms an integral part of the ensemble.

Although the two houses differ in size and are physically and functionally independent of each other, they are similar enough to make them appear as a single entity. The wide eaves protecting their façades, the metal windows and the modulation systems which form them, the combination of brick and stuccoed surfaces in the façades and the interiors, the polished concrete floors and the generous way in which the light penetrates each of the houses act as elements which, while not overlooking the necessary differences between them, enables recognition of the similarity which links them and establishes their value as an ensemble that evokes an order of city scale.

The serene and forceful simplicity of the exterior, which guarantees the relationship of the buildings to their noble surroundings, is set against the almost playful complexity of the inner spaces, with their restrained but expressively pleated surfaces and the well-conceived openings which frame the views of the outside in contrasting celebration of the site.

1 and 2 Sketches
Opposite page: View from the street

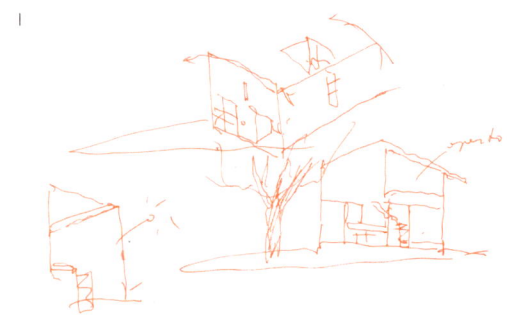

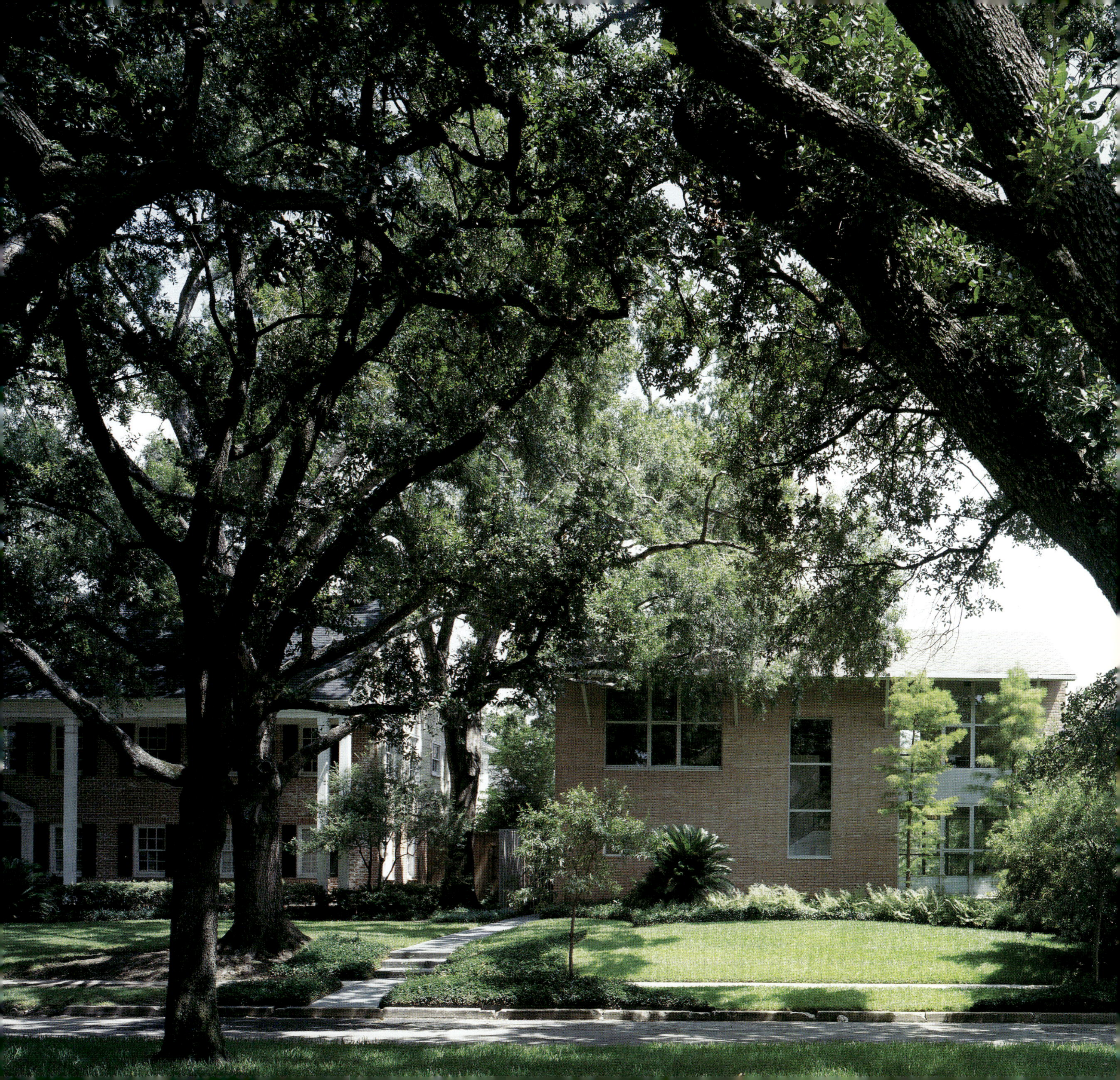

1 Partial view from the street
2 Cross section
3 and 4   Floor plans
5 Side façade
6 Main access

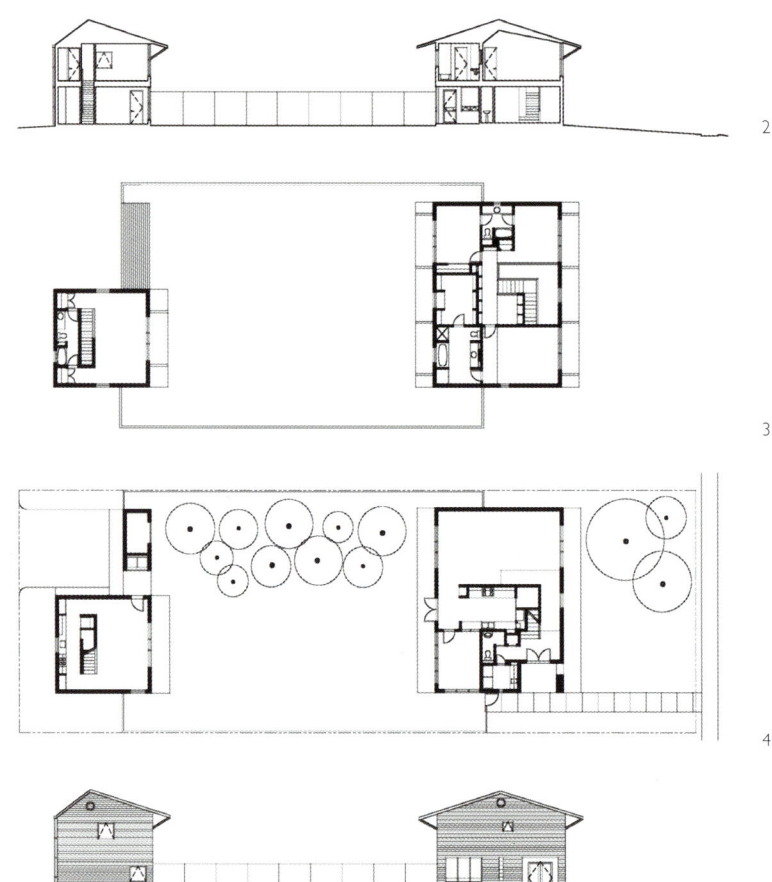

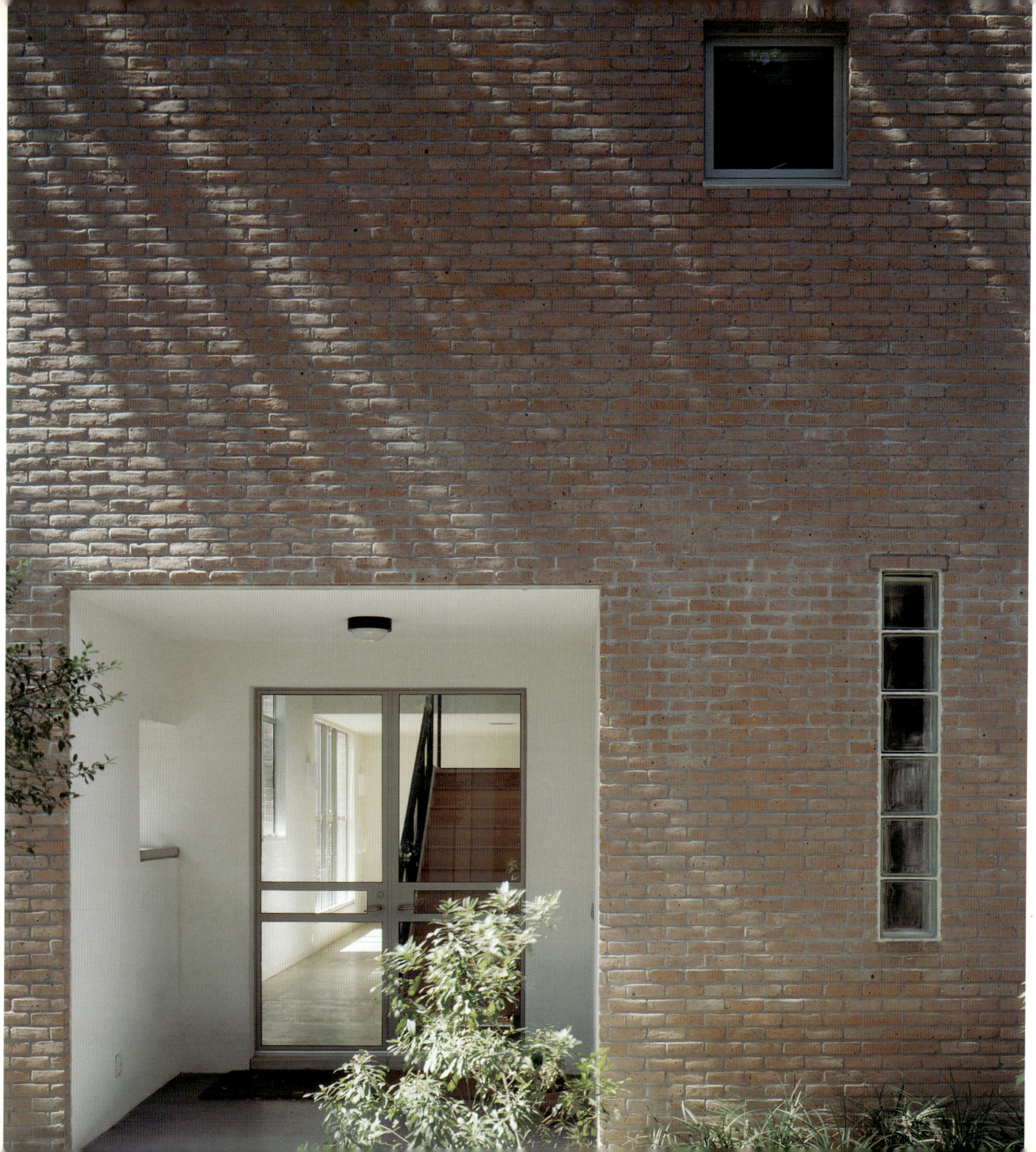

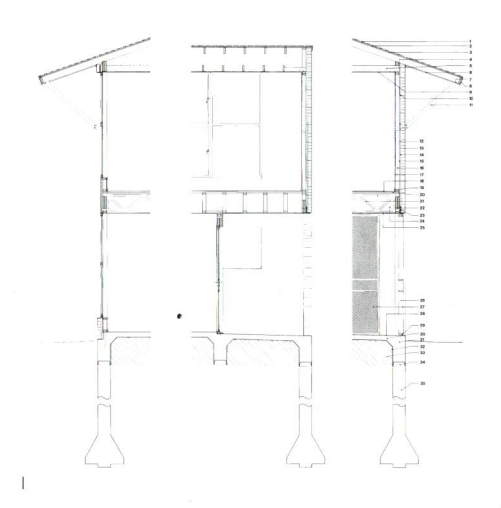

1 Building detail
2 Detail of the façade
3 View towards the main living room

3

1 Living room
2 Study
Opposite page: Detail of stairs

Lott House 53

House in La Barranca de San Isidro

San Isidro, Buenos Aires, Argentina
1984-1988

Francisco Billoch / Ignacio Dahl-Rocha / Juan Ignacio Ramos

Clients: *Christian and Claudia Schmiegelow*
Structures engineer: *Miguel Durlach*
Builder: *Madero and Lenhardson*
Photography: *Roberto Riverti*

In the San Isidro residential area, some 20 km north of the centre of Buenos Aires, the House in La Barranca is set against the cliff which defines the drop from the plains of the Pampas towards the River Plate. The house is built on a containing wall and with the superimposition of parallel layers of mass, walls, balconies and steps which descend with the slope. The solidity of the brick planes which envelop and hide the concrete structure emphasises the density of the masses, superimposed like bricks of a larger scale in an almost random manner climbing the slope to create gardens, terraces and varied balconies.

The relationship between the interior and the exterior, created by openings carved out of the masses with the eloquence of marked contrast, becomes dense and deep owing to the arrises of the windows, dealt with as layers of material which must be pierced in order to reach the space beyond. The persistent use of a single material, strongly modular and densely tectonic, arranged simply and almost without articulation, confers upon the house the overwhelming silence of the ethical conviction of the construction as both source and goal of architectural speculation.

In order to obtain the best views, the social areas of the house are placed on the upper level, which is reached by way of a plain but monumental stairway that starts in the block housing the bedrooms. Both have as their base the section housing the garages and service areas and against which are the wide steps leading to the entrance. The frontal character imposed by the plane of exposure to the views is counteracted by shifting the blocks parallel to the containing wall and the use of the sides as recreation areas.

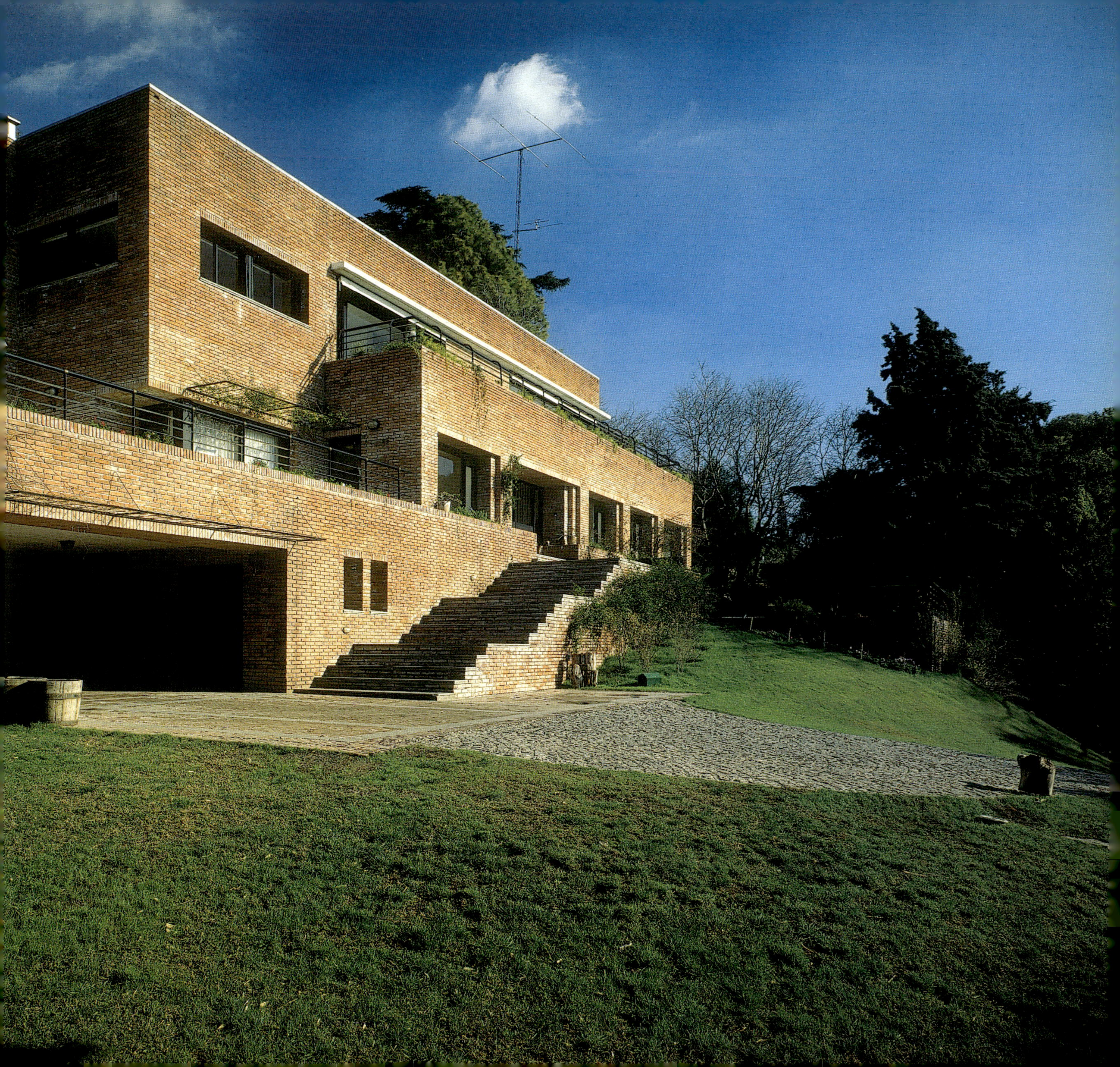

1　Sketch
2　Detail of section of the façade
3　View of the ensemble

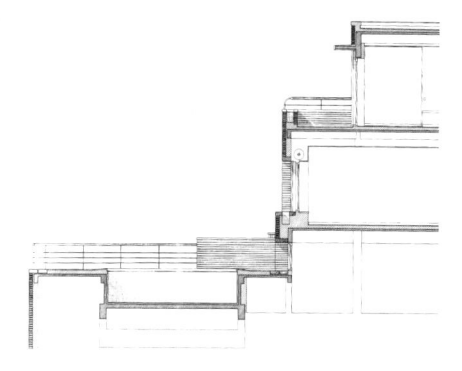

House in La Barranca

1 Upper floor
2 Garden and side terrace
3 View of the terrace towards the river

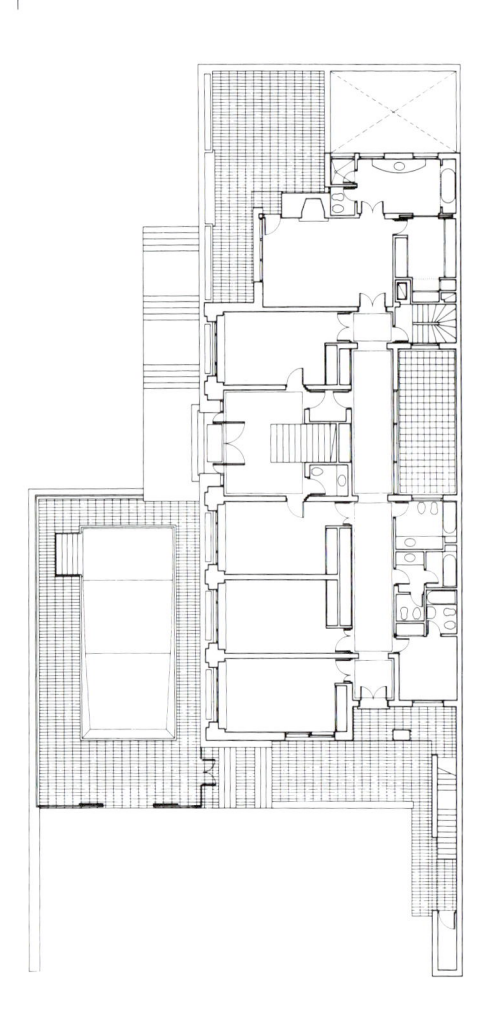

3

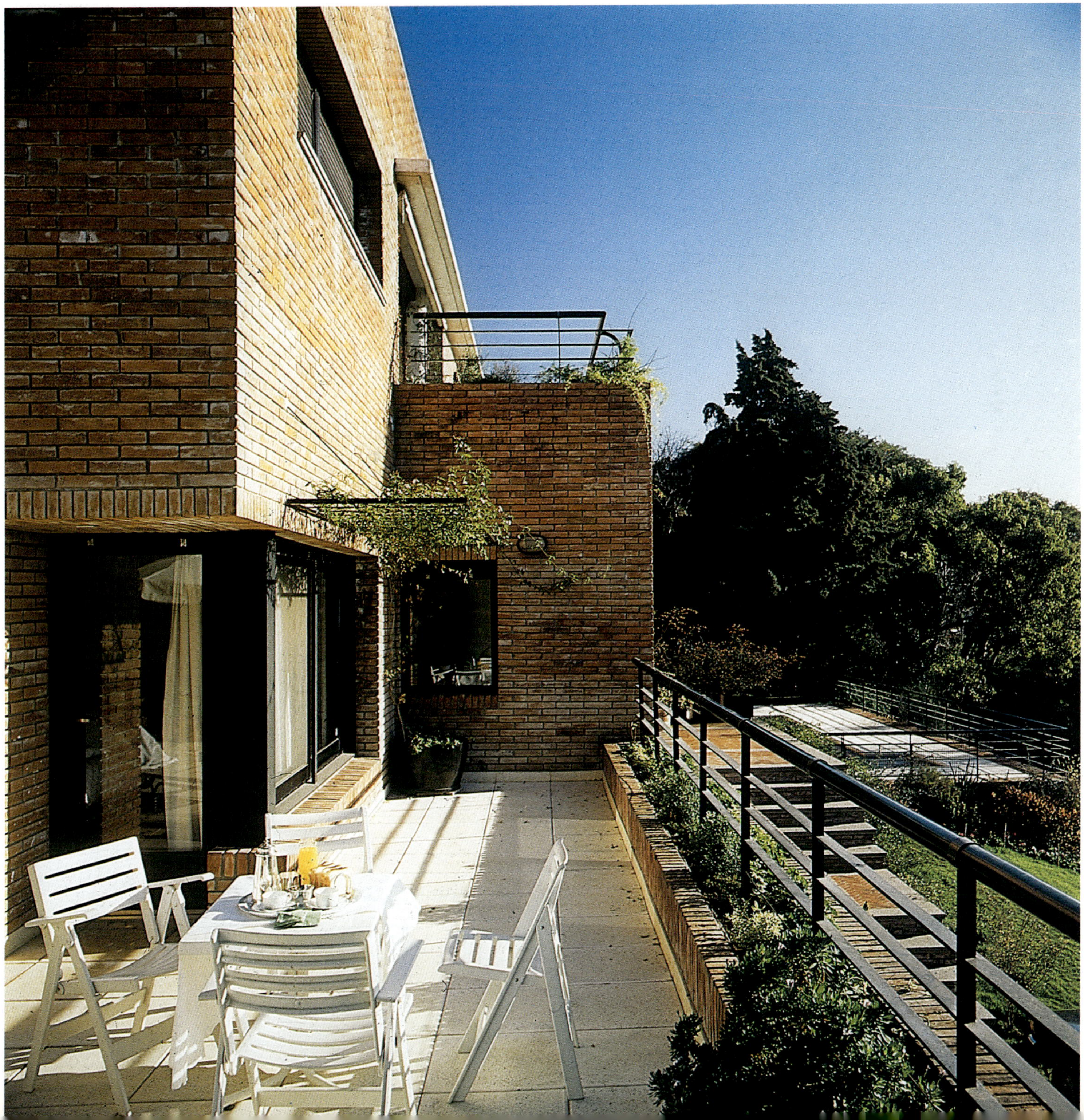

1 Interior staircase
2 Main living room
3 Detail of the façade

3

House in Córdoba
Quintas de San Antonio, Córdoba, Argentina
1994-1998

Leopoldo Laguinge

Structures: *Pedro Huerta, Ingeniero*
Photography: *Anselmo Pérez*

A plain stone block, this 110m x 55m villa in Córdoba, is set against the serene majesty of the sky of the Argentine Pampas and the orderly layout of the cultivated fields with their rectangular plots surrounded by poplar trees, their irrigation channels and the ploughed furrows mechanically shaping the landscape. Between the plains to the east and the blue outline of the mountains to the west, space here is not measured by the quantity of earth, but by the quantity of sky.

The abstract clarity of the geometry of the area pits its exactness against the overwhelming vastness of the territory. The reality of the house—with its solid stone walls, its large wooden doors, its thick concrete roofs suspended in the air—functions as an anchor of certainty against the infinite continuity of the landscape.

As a tangible refuge in the face of fear of uncontrollable scale, space in the house is judiciously arranged with limited but sensibly applied resources and the effectiveness of a well-planned distribution of the territory. The face of the building seen from the access offers just a few revealing openings. Behind that, and arranged in two bodies integrated by the continuity of the roof slats, the spaces follow the orthogonal lines of the reception area in a group of white boxes and patios which accommodate the activities of the house. A system of large wooden sliding doors providing contrast to allow the modification of the internal and external spaces interrelate with the silent force of the rest of the architectural resources employed. A water tower gives the only attempt at a silhouette. The distinct horizontal nature of the territory marks the deliberate articulation of the forms and the dominant continuity of the surfaces, finding materials which are in almost violent opposition to each other. A swimming pool is added to the landscape, thereby modulating the strips of lawn and the vegetable garden.

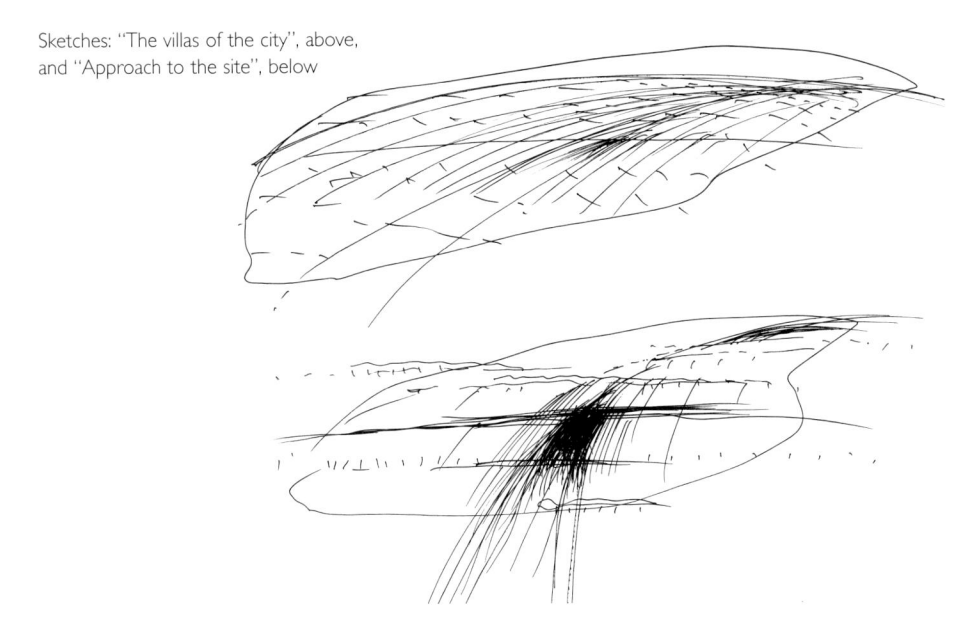

Sketches: "The villas of the city", above, and "Approach to the site", below

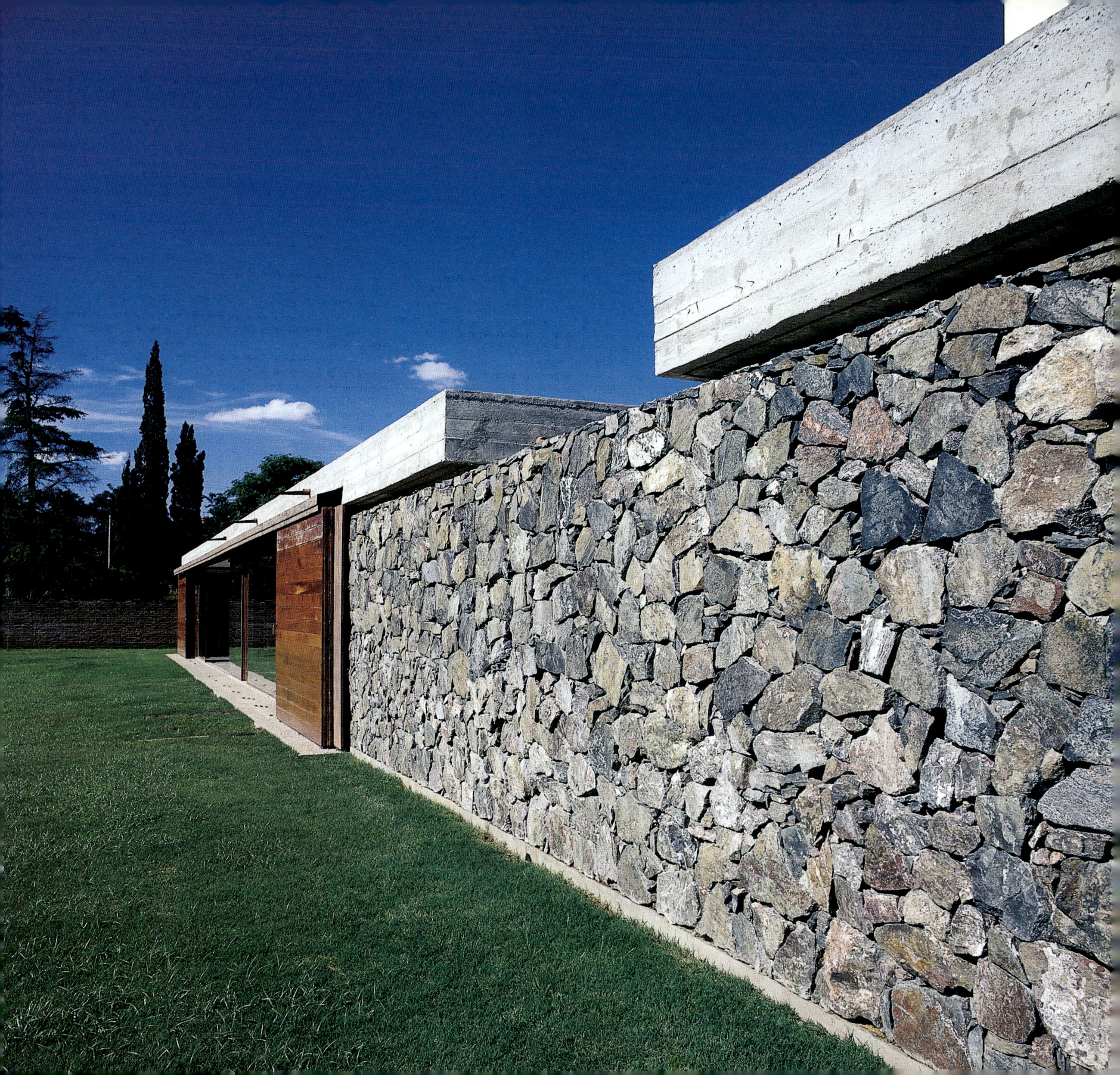

1 Floor plan
2 Cross section
3 Longitudinal section
Opposite page: View at night

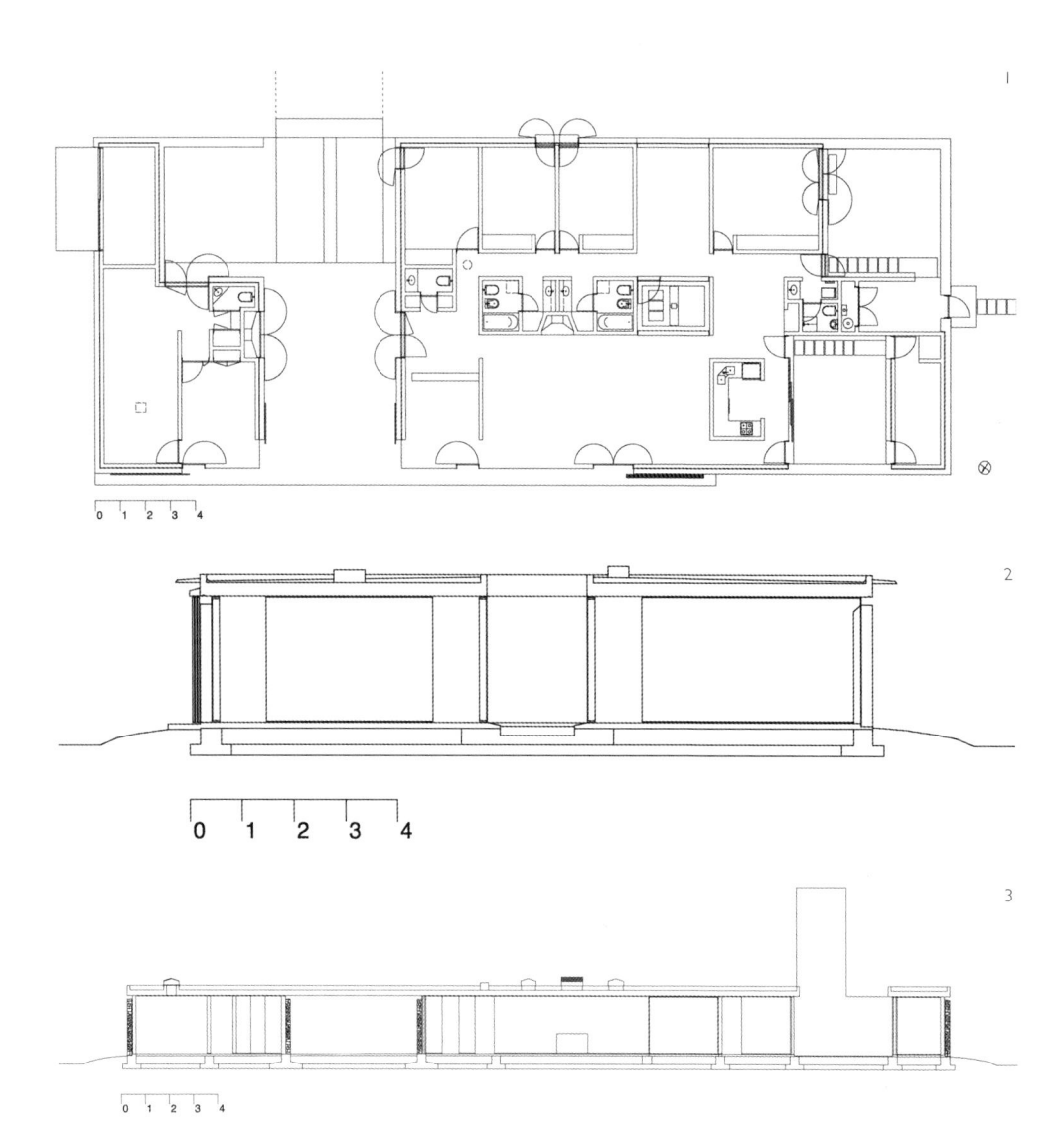

House in Córdoba

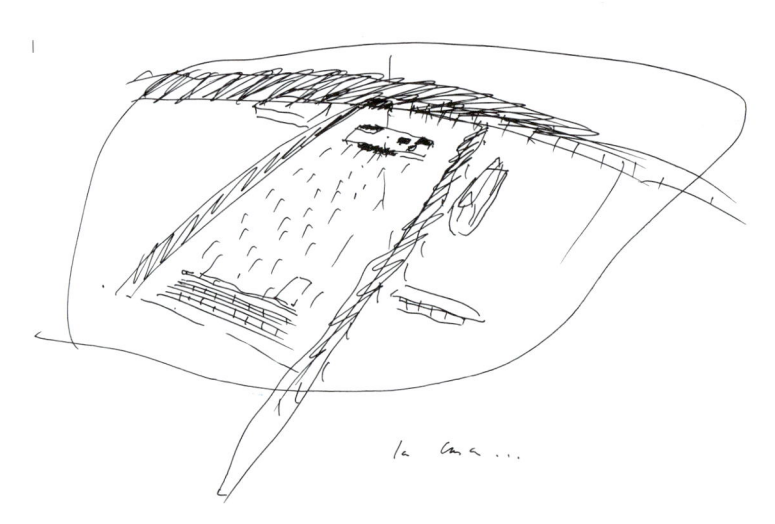

1 Sketch
2 View of the access

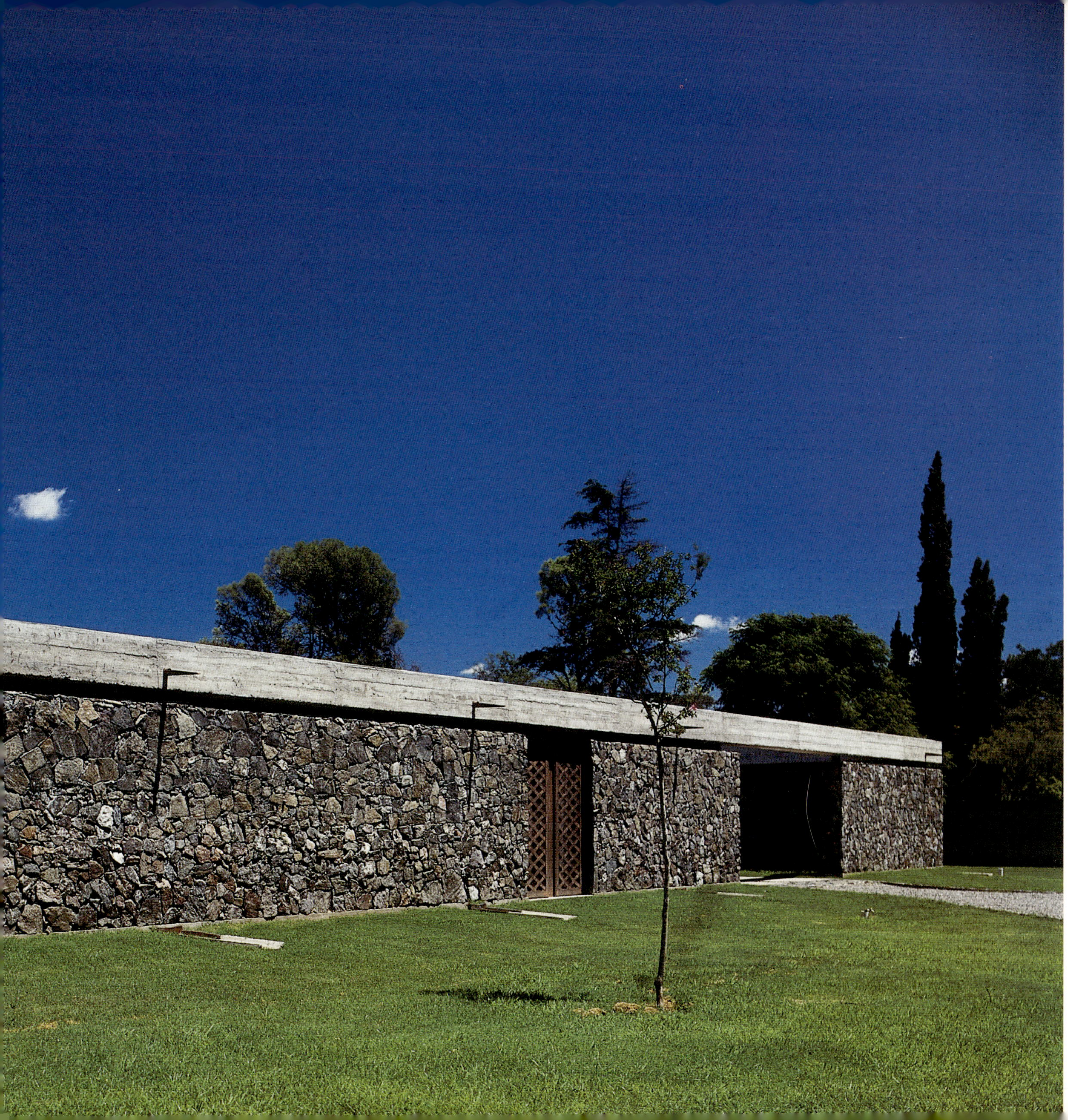

Floridia House

Miami, Florida, United States
1993-1995

María de la Guardia / Teófilo Victoria

Client: *Natasha Gottlieb / Francisco de Paula Victoria*
Architecture: *De la Guardia Victoria Architects / Trelles-Cabarrocas Architects*
Photography: *Southern Living, Inc. / Silvia Martin, photographer*

This house—inspired directly by Florida's vernacular cracker-style traditions—is in a semi-rural area, south of Miami. Making use of the more commonly available materials, this form of architecture, proposed in the case of this building as a project to evoke memory of the site, responds to the climatic conditions by using wide surfaces of shadow and intermediate space with simplicity.

The building is raised on stiles, thus enabling its easy identification as a space within the space, a refuge which contrasts harmoniously with the site's natural aggressive environment. A relatively solid body in the interior of the house is arranged symmetrically, enfolded by a ring of sheltered galleries which sets a quiet area apart for contemplation of the surrounding scene. The expressive use of both components creates a silhouette which is integrated, recognisable, family-orientated and of serene aspect; its most noteworthy feature being the centre with a high gable roof, covered with metal sheeting from the ridge down to the shallower eaves over the porches. The industrial pieces of regular and predetermined sizes serve to bring out the severe simplicity of the traditional architecture as well as to emphasise the subtle abstraction of forms and proportions. Thus by incorporating less conventional materials and a convincing mathematical order, a timeless atmosphere is given to the geometric regularity of the figures proposed as referential marks for the construction of memory.

In the interior, the central body is developed in a system of clearly defined spaces, articulated in a dense rhythm of compartments opening directly onto the porches. The contrast between the masonry walls of the main areas and the wooden partition walls in the bedrooms (the only closed spaces to invade the continuity of the perimeter galleries) makes plain the different authority of the parts in the silent and deliberate way which characterises the proposal as a whole.

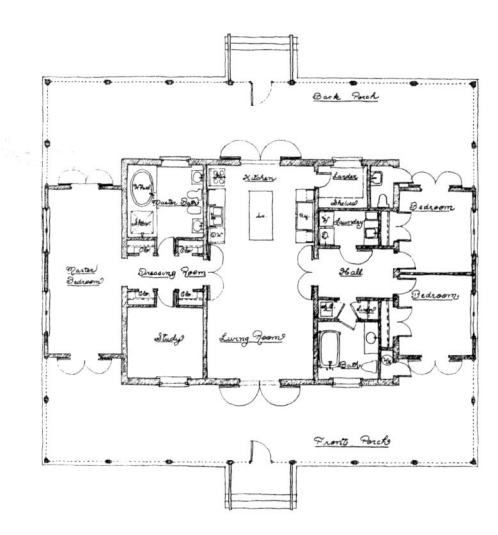

Floridia House 69

1 Detail of the porch
2 Section
3 Façade
Opposite page: Porch facing north

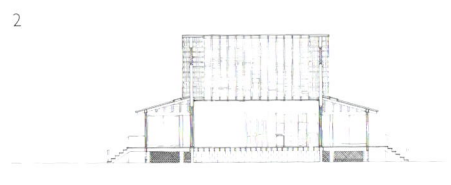

Floridia House 71

1 Porch facing east
2 Central living room
3 Main bedroom

Floridia House 73

House in La Barranca

Colonia del Sacramento, Uruguay
1996-1998

Mariano Clusellas / Horacio Baliero

Engineering: *Estudio de Ingeniería Cotto y Cheves*
Construction: *various craftsmen from Colonia del Sacramento*
Photography: *Gustavo Sosa Pinilla / Guido Chouela, Living*

1 Site plan
Opposite page: View of the access

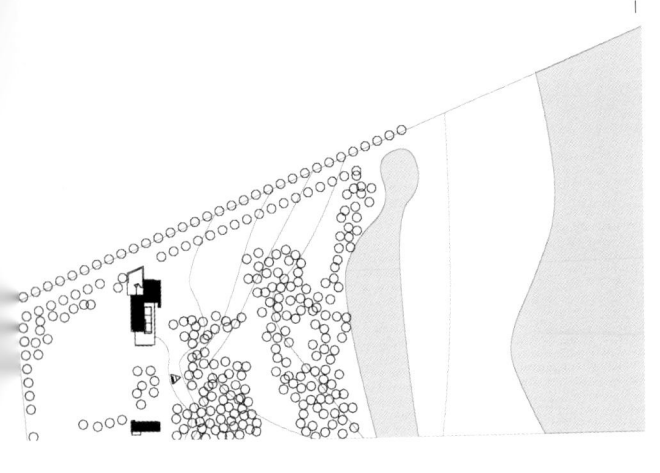

Ten kilometres from the old part of the city of Colonia del Sacramento stands the House in La Barranca at the point where the Argentine plain diverges from the leafy coastal jungle, marking the drop towards the immense River Plate. Seeming almost like an observation post, the site commands a remarkable view of the evening sun reflected in the river before disappearing into the water, in a dramatic contrast that seems to be crying out for action that would give a sense of habitation to such vastness. Onto this landscape of extremes, the architectural strategy arranges tangible situations which, with the evidence of their material and the allusions to their forms, construct memories on the site which seek to make it distinguishable.

An expanse of corrugated metallic sheet is the first image of the house seen on approach, placing the building firmly against the horizon. The almost craft-like figure of this sloping plane possesses the charm of a provisional and naked wilfulness, as does the dry surface of cactus and rustic materials over the entrance. Once entrance is gained, the space within is transformed into a transparent explosion of light which, passing between layers of glass, balconies, foliage and mosquito screens, seeks the river between the pillars and columns which frame the panorama in such a way as to make the natural environment appear almost within arm's reach.

Towards the north, the space spreads to a terrace with a swimming pool which, resting on a platform, runs parallel to the bedrooms and their auxiliary spaces contained between the corrugated metal plane, to define the silhouette of the roofs and the freer composition of the stone walls which project their visual strength over the terraces. The coming together of contrasting materials evokes the serene expressiveness of the austere vernacular architecture and the pioneering charm of the unusual.

Further away to the north, a tower / observation post / water tank rises up at the edge of the gorge.

House in La Barranca 75

1   View from the east
2, 3 and 4   Floor plans
5   Main living room

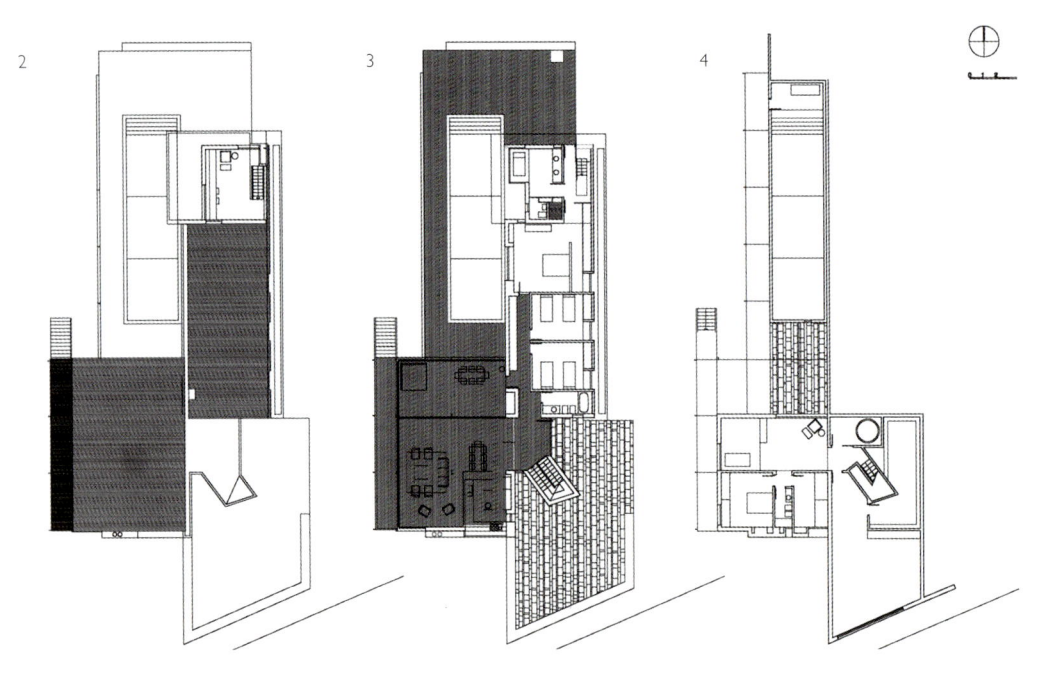

76

5

1 Main access
2, 3 and 4 Cross sections
5 Detail of the interior

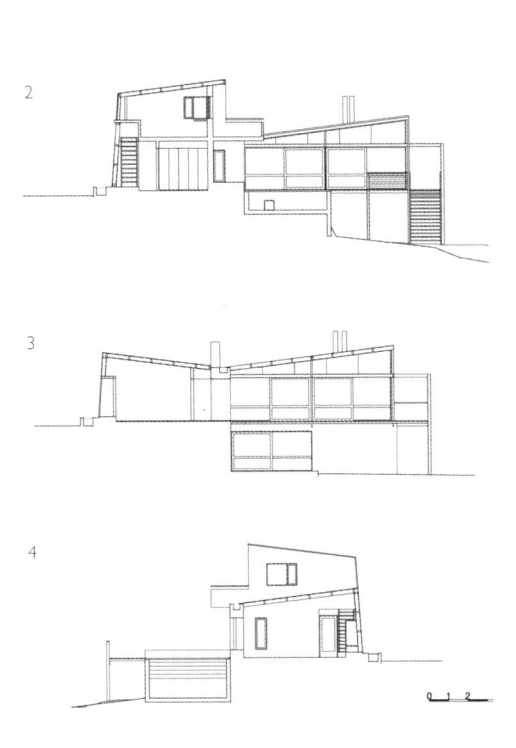

5

1 Construction details
2 View of the living room from the verandah
Opposite page: Terrace housing the swimming pool

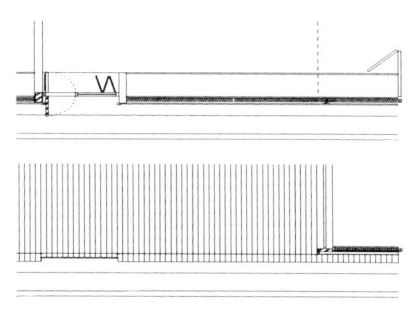

House in La Barranca

House on the Lake
Lake Carraizo, Trujillo Alto, Puerto Rico
1998-1999

Agrait Betancourt Arquitectos

Client: *Linda González / Vanessa Betancourt, Rebecca Betancourt / Marcos E. Betancourt / Bongo / Fiforita*
Architect: *Carlos Betancourt*
Partner in charge: *Carlos E. Betancourt LLambías*
Architect in charge: *Jesús G. Maldonado*
Collaborator: *Mario J. Dumont / Antonio García*
Drawing: *Boris W. Díaz*
Consultants:
    Civil Engineering: *Jesús M. Suárez*
    Structure: *David McCloskey / Daniel León*
    Plumbing: *Pedro Medina*
    Electrical installations: *Leonardo Vidal*
Contractor: *SM Contractor / Samuel Morales Resto / All Steal Service / Franky Vásquez*
Photography: *Ivonne María Marcial / Fabián S. Morales*

The house is sited on a rocky, wooded peninsula which slopes steeply down towards an artificial lake that dominates the landscape. The concentration of trees creates dense and impenetrable surroundings of marked verticality in contrast to the expansive horizontality of the lake. Constructed with materials which refer to the site—as if the building were just one more piece of the surroundings, modulating their best moments and hierarchies—the architecture of this open refuge is an orderly arrangement of a group of concrete walls within which a compartment of steel and wood houses the domestic activities.

A winding path leads up to the *meseta* or tableland upon which the building is sited. The almost solid concrete block frames the views with its pillars and openings. The groundfloor contains the maintenance and utilities area, as well as a gallery for leisure use. Above that, at access level, are the social areas, arranged as a continuous space and open towards the north by means of a platform which extends towards the interior landscape of the wooded area, and towards the splendour of the view of the lake through four large wooden windows.

The stairway which flanks the eastern edge of the house leads—in an attractive play of concrete planes, colour, lights and visions suggested by the half-open corners—to the bedrooms on the upper level. In the bedrooms, the same range of materials, on a smaller scale and with plainer surfaces, expresses the variation in character of the rooms without injecting a discordant note. The roof, of zinc sheets on wooden beams, shelters the house with its eaves and enfolds it within the virtual plane formed together with the wooden pillars on the south face.

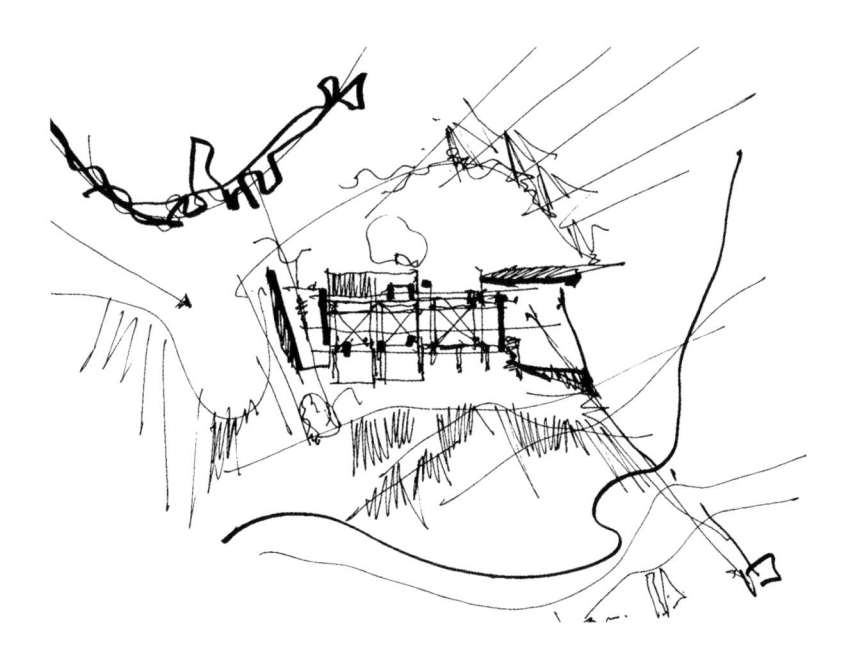

House on the Lake 83

1 Site plan
2 Aerial view
3 Floor plan of the first level
4 Floor plan of the second level
5 View from the north-east

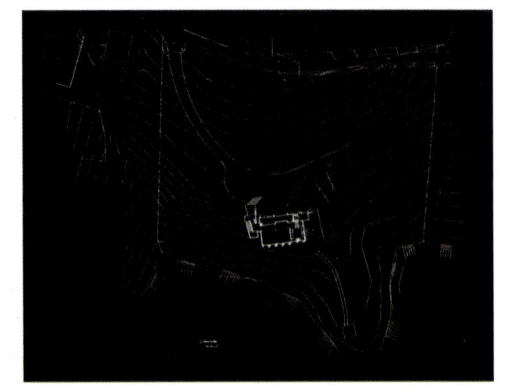

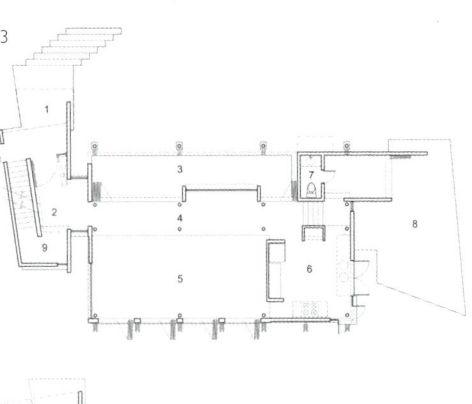

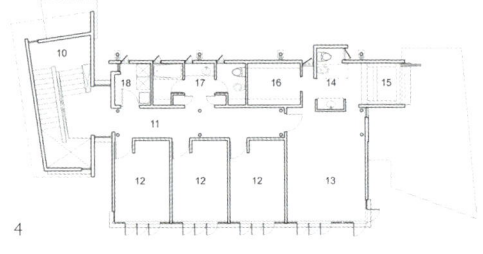

House on the Lake

1

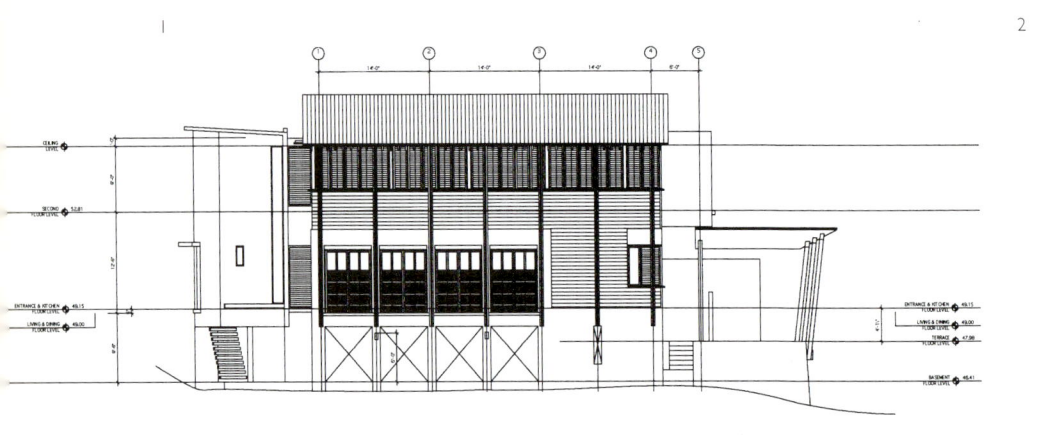

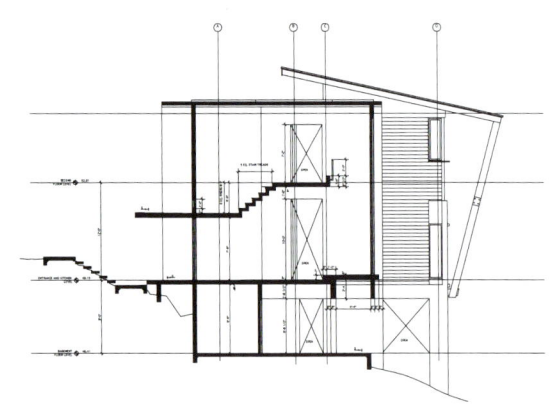

2

3

86

1 Façade towards the lake
2 Cross section
3 Main living room
4 View of the interior stairs towards the bedrooms

1 General view of the main living room
2 Bedroom
3 Detail of the living room

House on the Lake 89

House in Las Lomas de la Lagunita

Caracas, Venezuela
1993-1996

Enrique Larrañaga / Vilma Obadía

Client: *Inversiones Aldebarán C.A.*
Architecture: *Larrañaga-Obadía, Arquitectos & Asociados, C.A. / Susana Balbes, assistant*
Structure: *José Enrique Hererra*
Electricity / hydraulics: *Gaspar Arancibia*
Construction: *Promotora Aldebarán C.A. / Engineer Luis Andrés Lyon*
Photography: *Ado Iacobelli / Vilma Obadía / Reinaldo Armas / Enrique Larrañaga*

The transposition of the traditional urban house, built around a patio, to the suburban environment on the outskirts of Caracas leads us to examine the contrasts and possible complements between the centre of the typical dwelling and the expansive territorial space of the garden city. The way all the activities of the house go back to the patio creates a marked sense of cohesion, set against a series of almost autonomous forms, assembled as a collection of pieces, and the unobstructed and continuous relationship of the spaces with the exterior.

The lower level contains the common activities of the house, concentrated around the central patio in accordance with an elemental pattern of functional compartmentalisation. As the surfaces which enclose the living room and dining room are progressively dissolved, their spaces are extended into the outside garden. This garden, which envelops the house, reappears on the upper level, where the bedrooms are located; it acts as a haven of rest and relaxation and also contains the swimming pool, which extends towards the horizon and refers once again to the figure of the patio, that reappears as a centralising and cohesive element of domestic order.

Upon entering the house, the patio serves as the stage upon which all of the pieces converge, thereby evoking an urban presence. On the outside, masses are organised as incomplete sections of figures alluding to the solidity of the traditional wall—the profiles of the roofs, the eaves of the corridors, balconies and turrets. From the upper garden, the same forms appear with a different scale which alters the way they are perceived. In all cases, colour is incorporated as a compositional resource in order to differentiate the pieces, articulate relationships and characterise spaces. The modulation of the stretches of glass introduces an allusive decorative density, while the designs of the floor seek to provide continuity to the surfaces and emphasise the fluidity of the space.

1 Sketch
Opposite page: View from the main garden

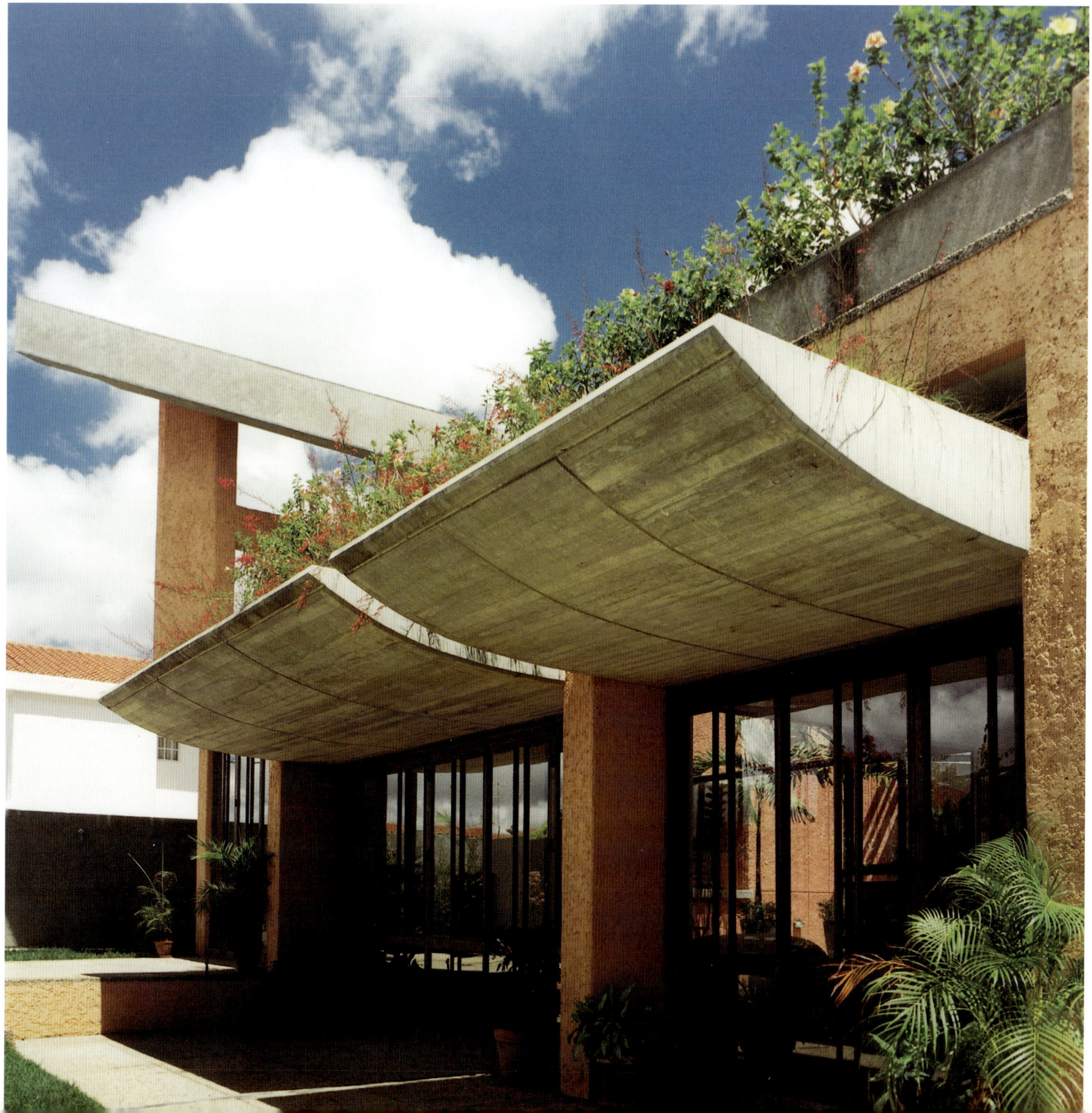

1 Interior patio, view towards the living room
2 Isometric section
Opposite page: View of the outside

2

92

House in Las Lomas de la Lagunita 93

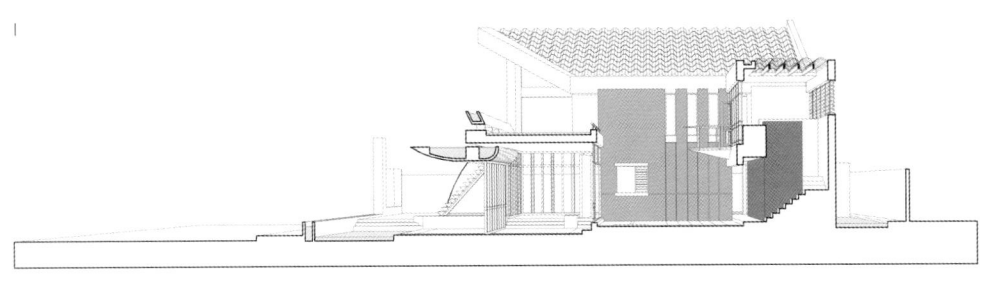

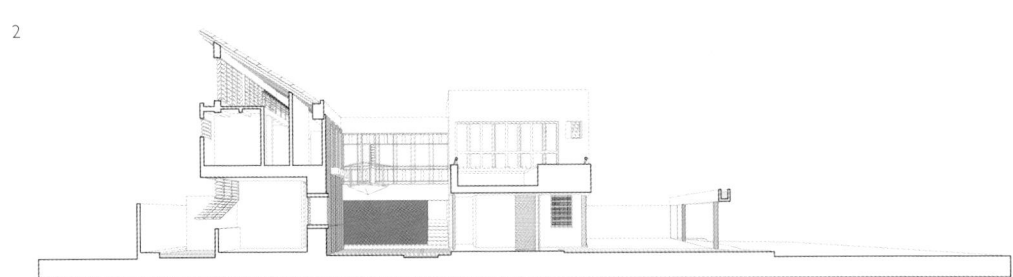

1 Longitudinal section
2 Cross section
3 Balcony overlooking the interior patio
Opposite page: Façade towards the east
Following double page: View of the upper garden seen from the swimming pool and of the canopies towards the garden

House in Las Lomas de la Lagunita 95

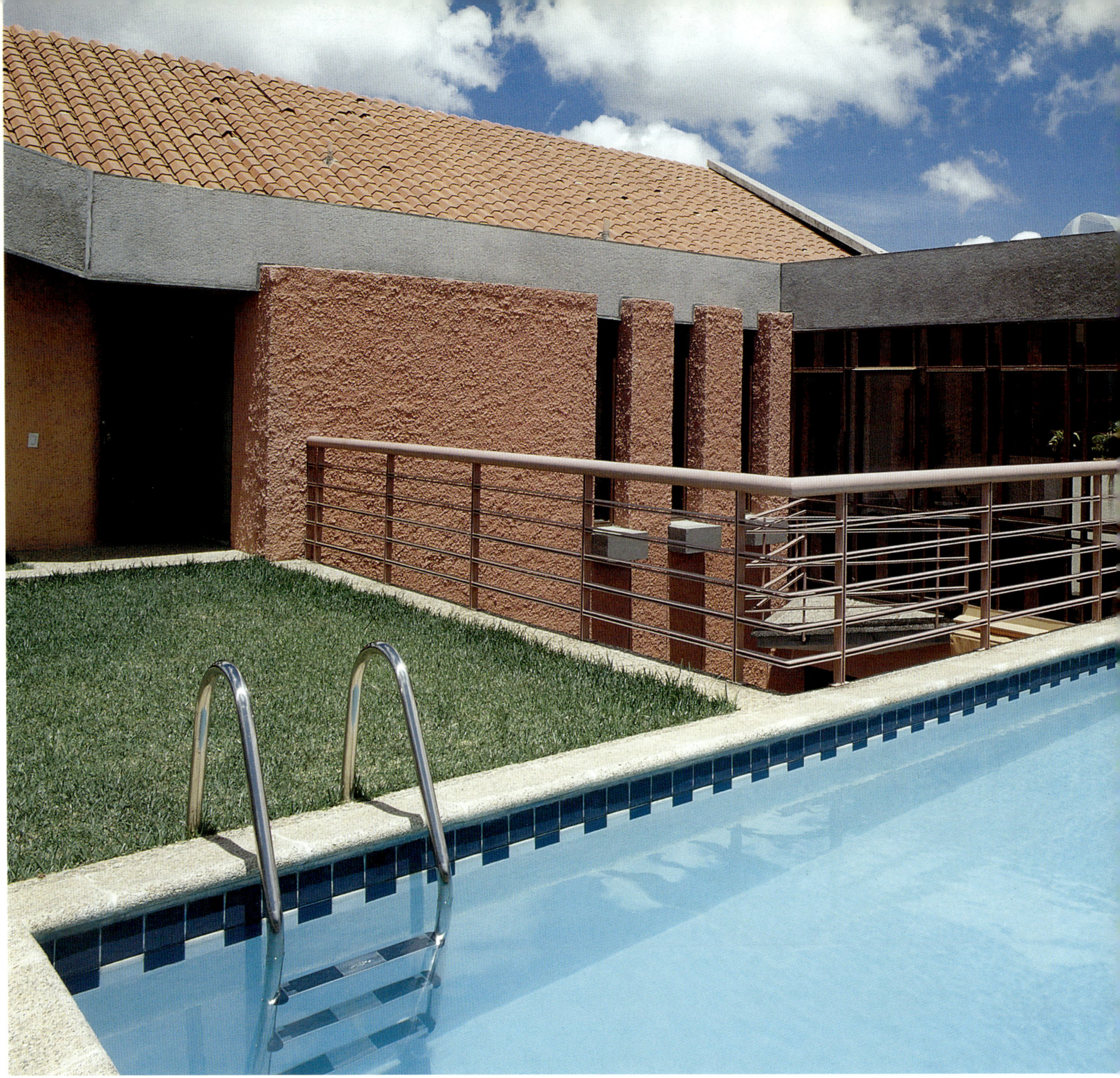

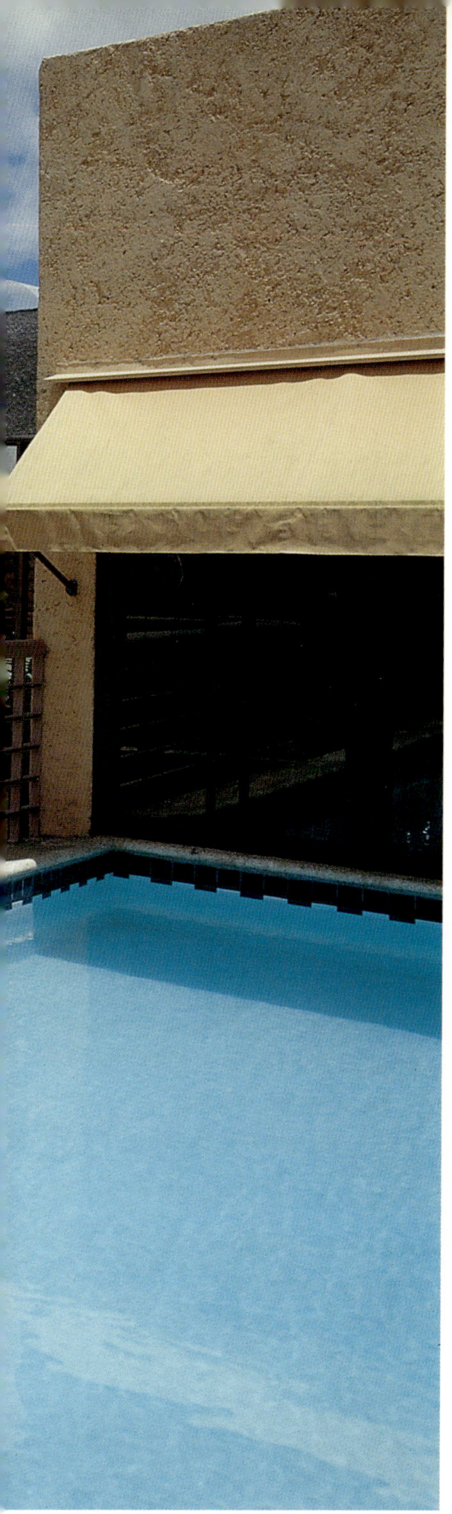
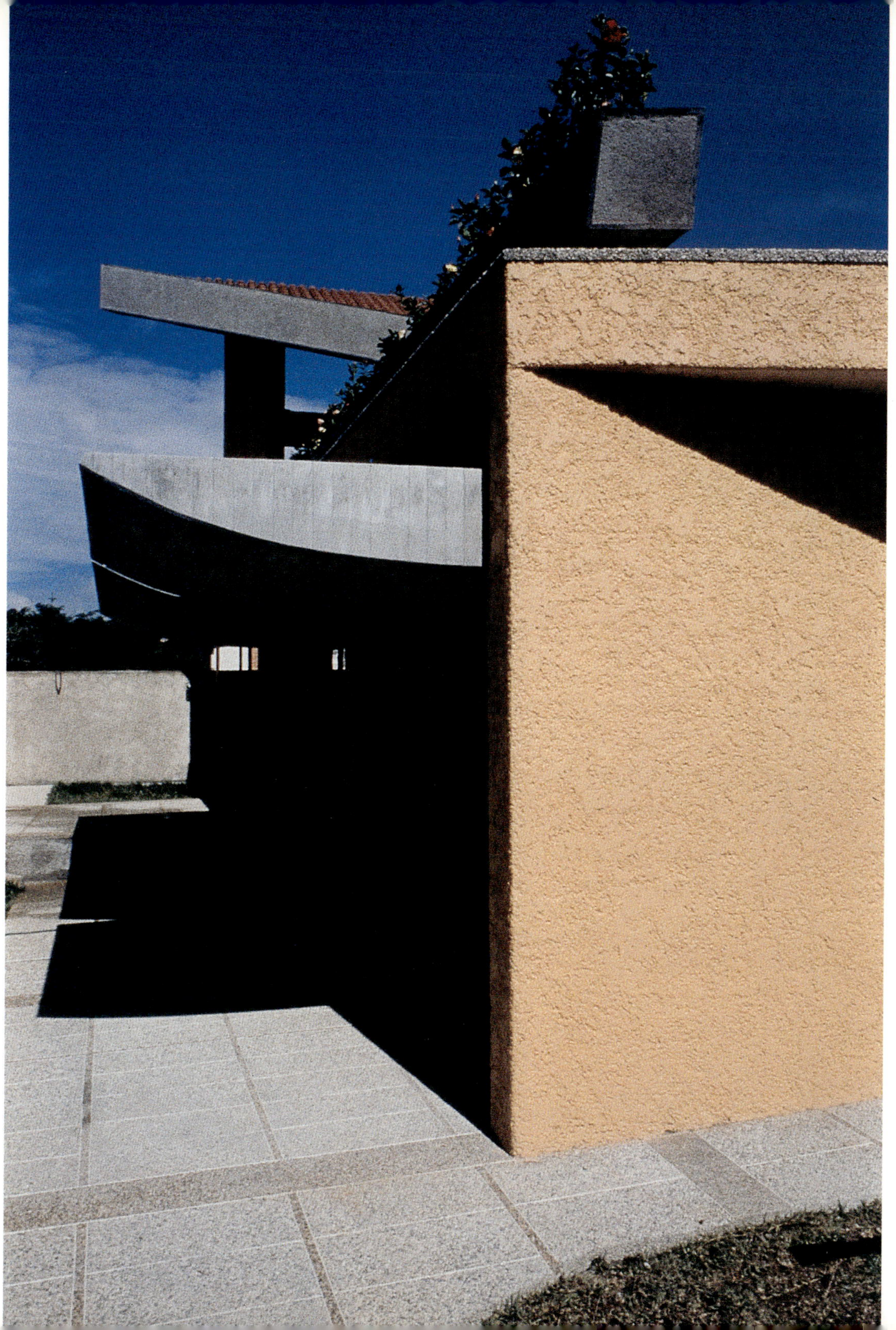

La Queja House

Cali, Colombia
1992-1998

Benjamín Barney-Caldas

Client: *Sylvia Vera Patiño Spitzer*
Project: *Benjamín Barney-Caldas, Architect*
Structural consultant: *Primo Andrés Cajiado, Engineer*
Construction (1992): *Jaime Beltran Vanegas, Architect*
Contractor (1994): *Pablo Saldaña*
Between 1996-98 and 2000: *Benjamín Barney-Caldas, Architect*
Master: *Ildefonso Quevedo*
Carpentry: *Isidro Gómez*
Ironwork: *Miguel Meneces*
Elevation and drawing: *Carlos Zapata*
Photography: *Sylvia Patiño*

The recovery of a site in an area of Cali—heavily affected by urban renewal operations that broke up the spatial structure of the neighbourhood—became an exploration of the traditional domestic order and the basis of an argument which gives priority to typological veracity over functional schematics.

Over a period of several years of work on site, with the owner and the builders working closely together, an organisational strategy was identified which, while respecting historical principles, allowed for a certain poetic and even aggressive licence, as witnessed by the ironic reference made by the name of the house to the persistent complaints of the neighbours regarding the proposed interventions ("*queja*" is the Spanish word for "complaint").

On a deep and narrow site, typical of the traditional town centres, the house is developed as a succession of similar pavilions and diverse patios which interweave interior and exterior and in which the different rooms are set. The compactness of the living quarters outlines the rhythmic openness of the successive empty spaces of air and light, just as the ever-changing fragility of the water contrasts with the solidity and roughness of the walls.

The original surfaces have been plastered and painted white, while the new buildings are made of concrete and projecting blocks, in an almost didactic manifestation of a spatial palimpsest temporarily superimposed.

The generous height of the rooms, the transformation of the spaces by means of corridors and galleries, the continual presence of the sky framed by the clear outlines of the patio, and the precise contrast of textures—all combine to produce a spatiality as compact as it is fluid. In a way this is at the same time both crude and refined, using forms and scales which allude to the tradition of the site without avoiding the abstract power of something evidently modern, and suggests an ambiguous temporality, contemporary complexity and traditional serenity.

1 Façade towards the street
Opposite page: View of the fifth patio

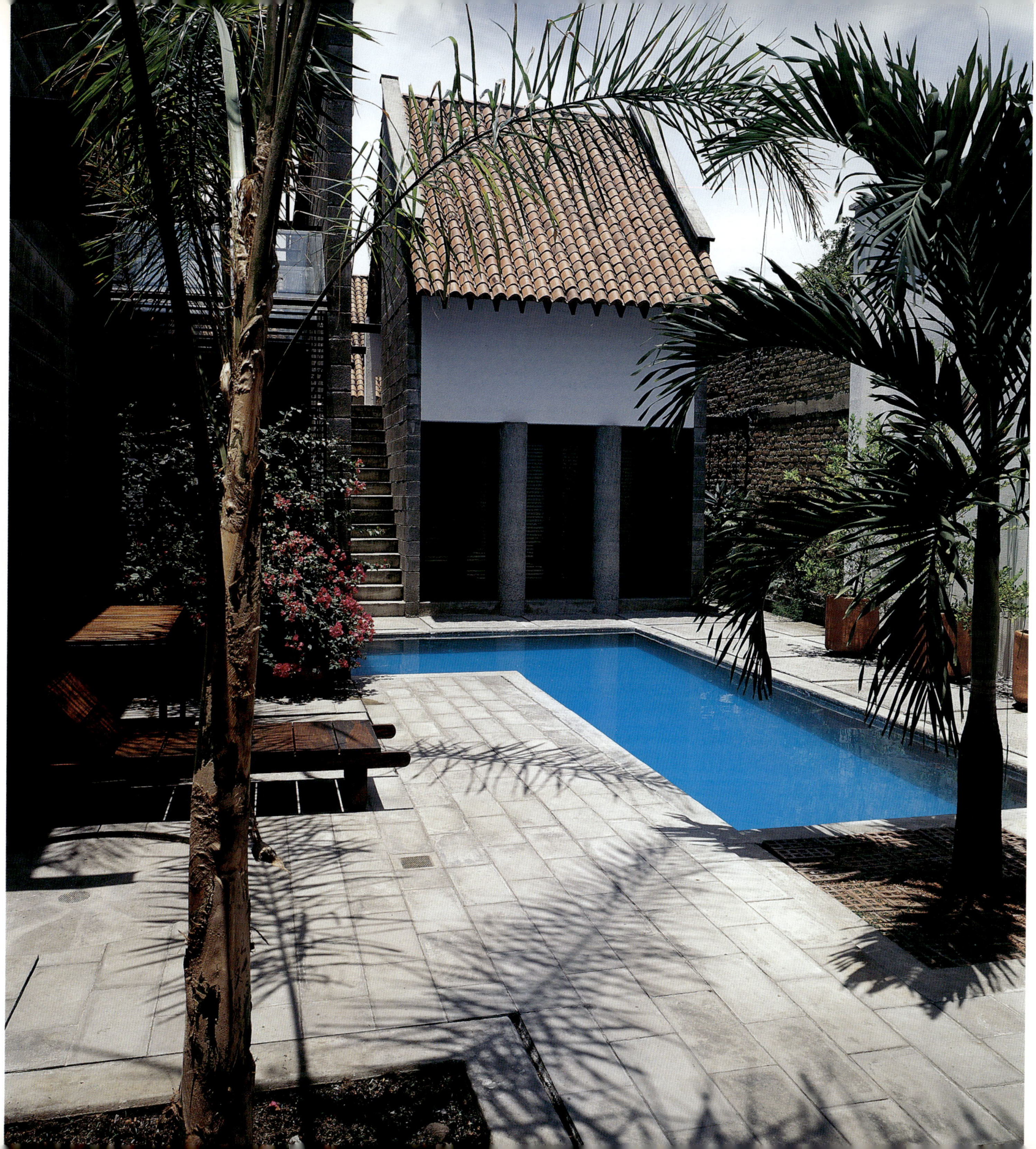

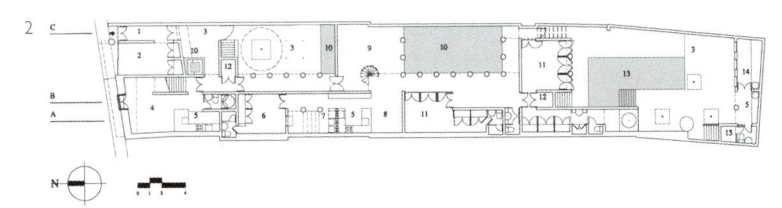

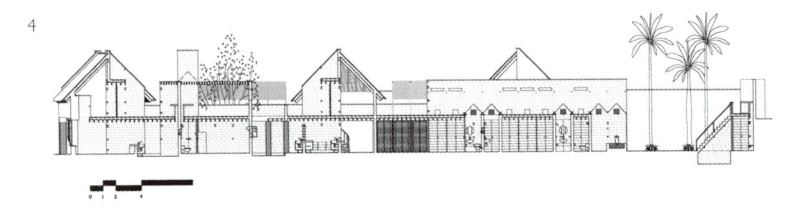

1 and 2 Floor plans
3 Fourth patio
4 Longitudinal section
5 Corridor

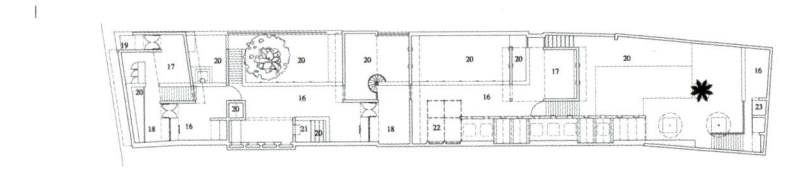

La Queja House 101

1 Main bedroom
2 Patio
3 Detail of the pond in the patio

2

3

Casabe House

Choroní, Aragua State, Venezuela
1995-1996

Ana Loreto

Client: *Diego Texera / Marianella Granados*
Structural Consultants: *Gladys Maggi / Fermín Valladares*
Wood technology consultant: *Urbano Ripoll*
Electrical consultant: *Luis Augusto Quintanales*
Construction: *Diego Texera / Alexis Pedrá*
Sanitary installations: *Ana Loreto*
Drawing: *Argenis Lugo / Mary Ruth Jiménez*
Photography: *Luis Brito / Gustavo Marcano*

1 Site plan
2 General floor plan

Opposite page: Panoramic view of the exterior

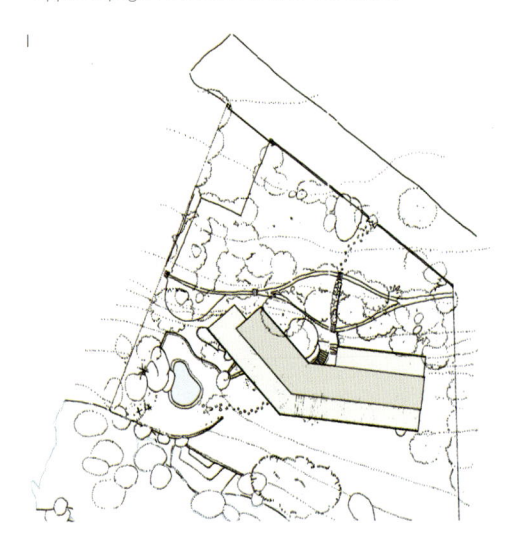

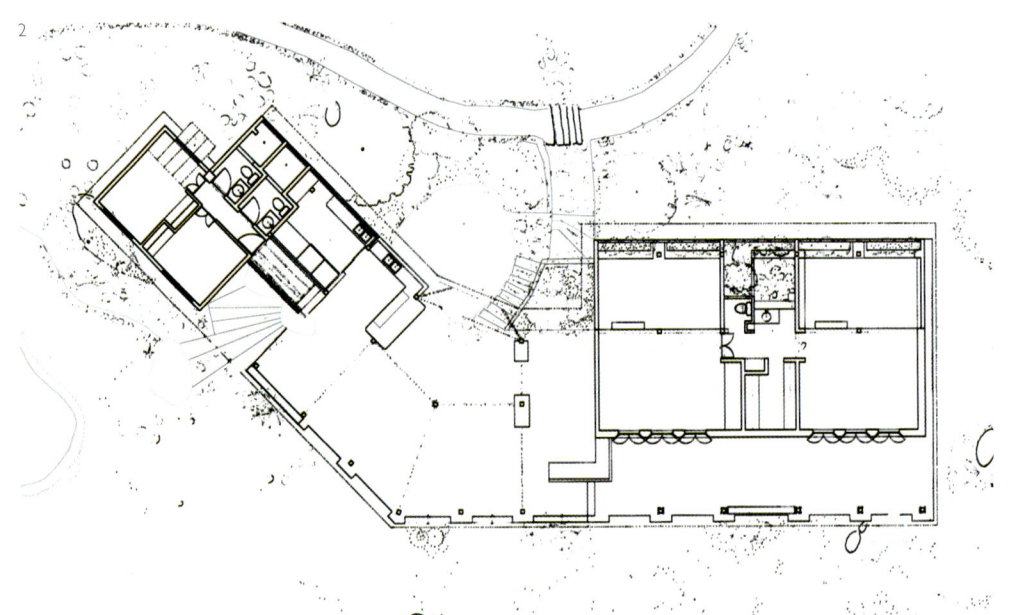

The Casabe House is in the coastal village of Choroní, whose local economy was originally based on cocoa; now, Choroní is a major tourist resort. From the city of Maracay the village is reached by crossing the lush tropical jungle of the coastal mountain range.

A young couple requested a house for permanent residence which would adapt itself to the existing environment of the site, which would be "habitable" and in which design and construction would constitute a single process. The aim was to recapture the unity between living and inhabiting, between designing and building, and integrate them into the experience of both the fascinating tropical foliage, wet with dew and interlaced with rivers and springs, and the proximity of the Caribbean Sea.

To begin this project—which was not designed to attract passing attention from outsiders (what's more, it lacks any façades)—it was necessary to study the site in depth, to include movement in the perception of it, to define a system of graphic indications for communication between the architect and the inhabitants, to develop a constructive dialogue which allowed spaces and techniques to be modified, added to and eliminated successfully to create the house, as if—in the resulting process of gestation and mutual enrichment—the architecture would become part of human communication.

In this shaded area, nature is ever present, containing almost imperceptibly the human act of building a house. The terrain acquires the consistency of the smooth cement of the floors; the roof of woven palms, moving like a leaf in the wind, offers the protective shade which would otherwise be provided by the trees; walls, curtains and wicket gates offer the privacy previously ensured by the undergrowth; rocks, promontories and slopes are part of the house, while the roof beams and eaves inhabit the ground like an alternative topography. In this architecture of subtle transitions we know what the inside is and where the outside is, but the line is blurred where the architecture itself begins.

Alberto Sato, Caracas, 2001

Casabe House

1
2

106

1 Main space seen from the bedroom area
2 Cross section of the access area
3 Cross section of the bedroom area
4 Main space seen from the service area

Casabe House 107

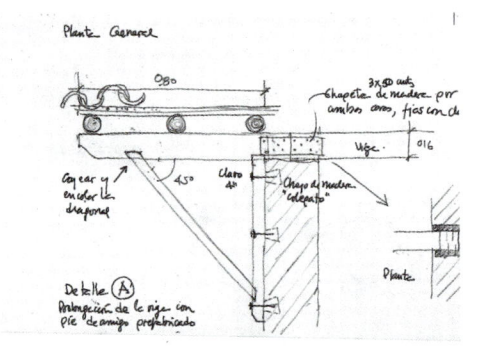

1 Sketch of the wooden structure
2 Bedroom
3 Cane roofs

3

D'Alessandro House

Carapicuiba, Sao Paulo, Brazil
1997-1998

Vinicius de Andrade / Marcelo Morettin

Client: *Paulo D'Alessandro / Domitila Coelho*
Design team: *Vinicius de Andrade / Marcelo Morettin, Project architects / J. G. da Silveira / J. E. Alves*
Wooden structure: *ITA: Helio Olga*
Contractor: *J. Francisco Chaves*
Photography: *Nelson Kon*

This small house close to a lake, on an extensive tree-covered site on the outskirts of Sao Paulo, is the home of a young couple, both of whom are photographers. The poetical power, clarity of form and material force of this primordial presence is clearly linked with the myth of the "primitive hut" and its purpose of interpreting simply, powerfully and essentially the complex immediacy of living.

The functions of the house are divided into two clear and opposing categories, related in a manner direct and elemental. The living and sleeping area is housed in an integrated and luminous space, by a wooden structure which supports the walls of polycarbonate panels and a roof of thermoacoustic metal tiles. A removable curtain enables fragile and occasional delimitation of the sleeping area and a corner window converts the landscape into an object of contemplation. The service areas are housed in a compact, closed volume of brick and concrete, containing small differentiated rooms which house the necessary facilities.

Built on a brick base, the main space of the house is presented in its surroundings as a form which is at the same time abstract and tangible, stark and modest, opposing the landscape as a manifestation of human will and also in harmony with it in the serenity of the specific reality. A wooden platform marks the area in the space that leads to the door. The translucent walls enable constant awareness of the exterior from within the house and of the domestic scene from without. The shadows and moving shapes animate and decorate the surfaces of the lighting box, producing with different levels of transparency and luminosity different readings of the architectural object.

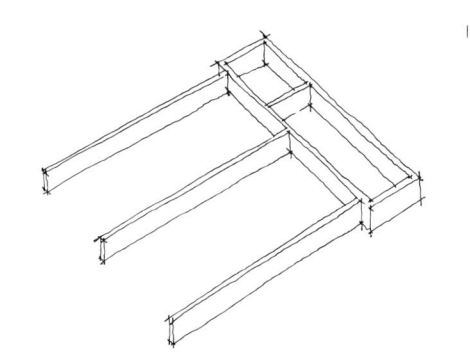

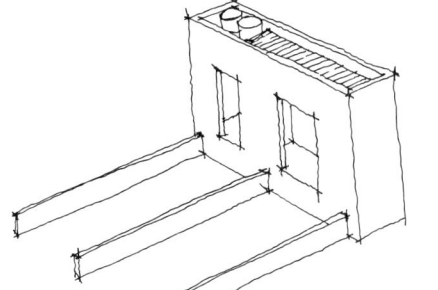

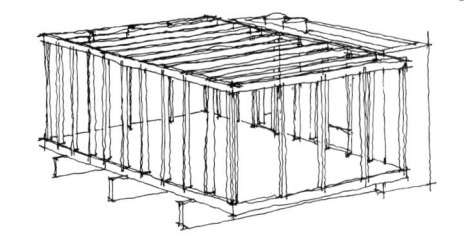

1 Sketch of the foundations
2 Sketch of the service area
3 Sketch of the structure
Opposite page: General view

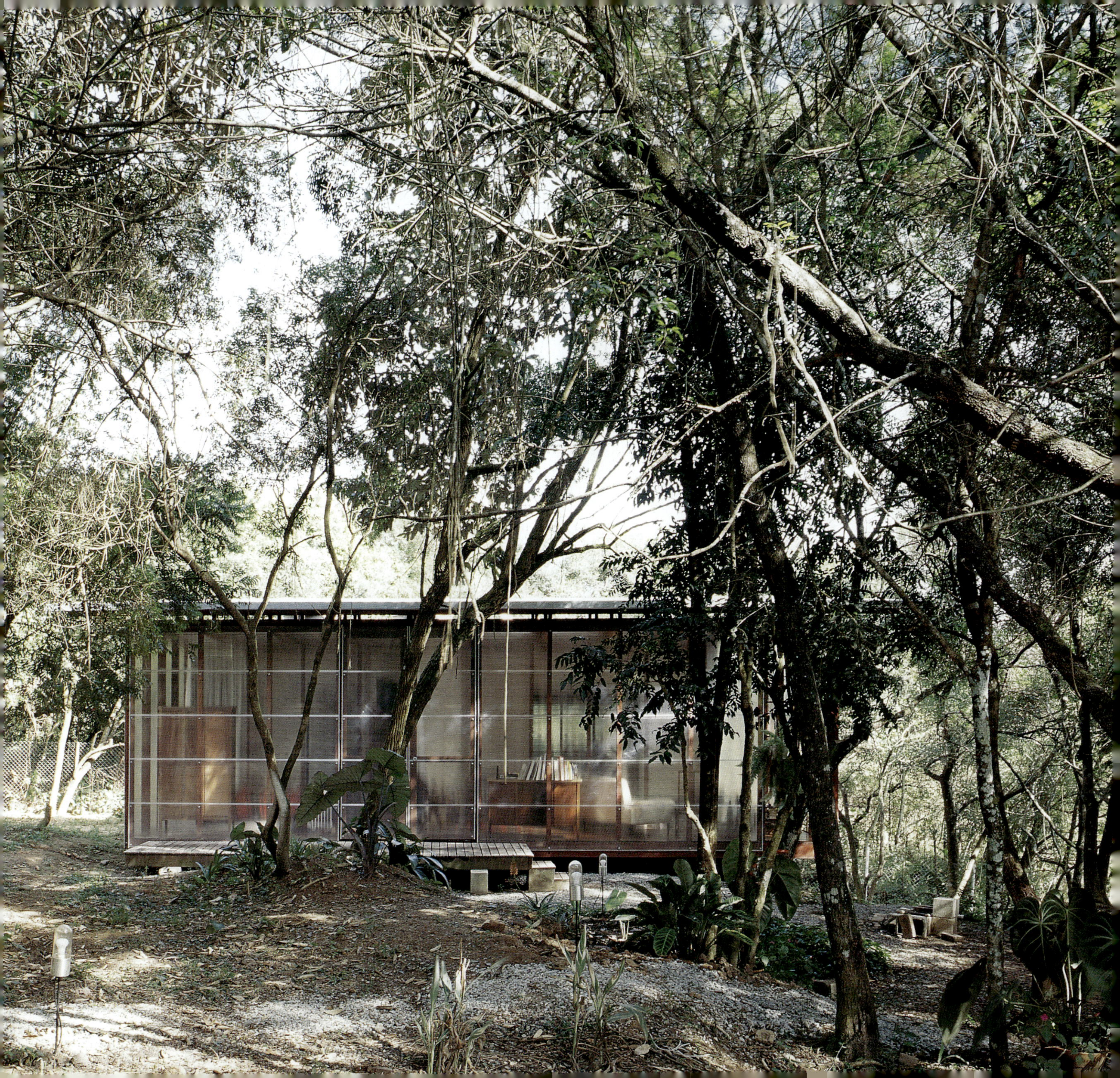

1 and 5   Façade towards the east
2   Interior living room
3 and 4   Façade towards the north
6   Floor plan
Following pages: View of the eastern access

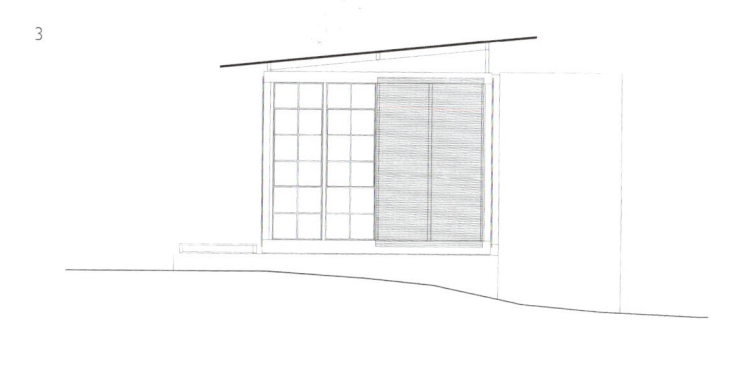

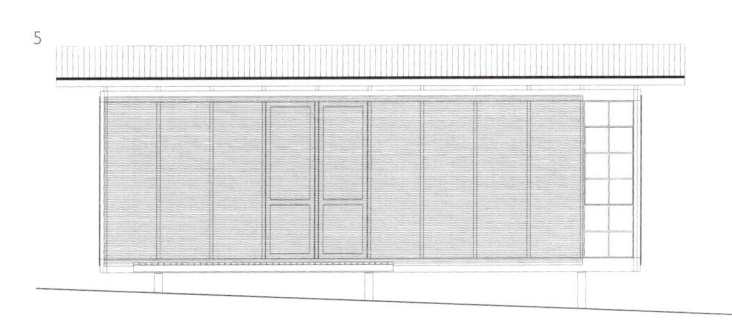

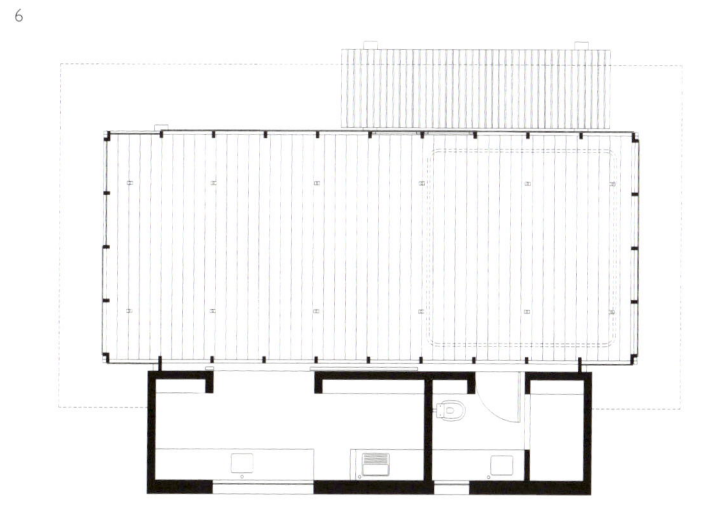

D'Alessandro House 113

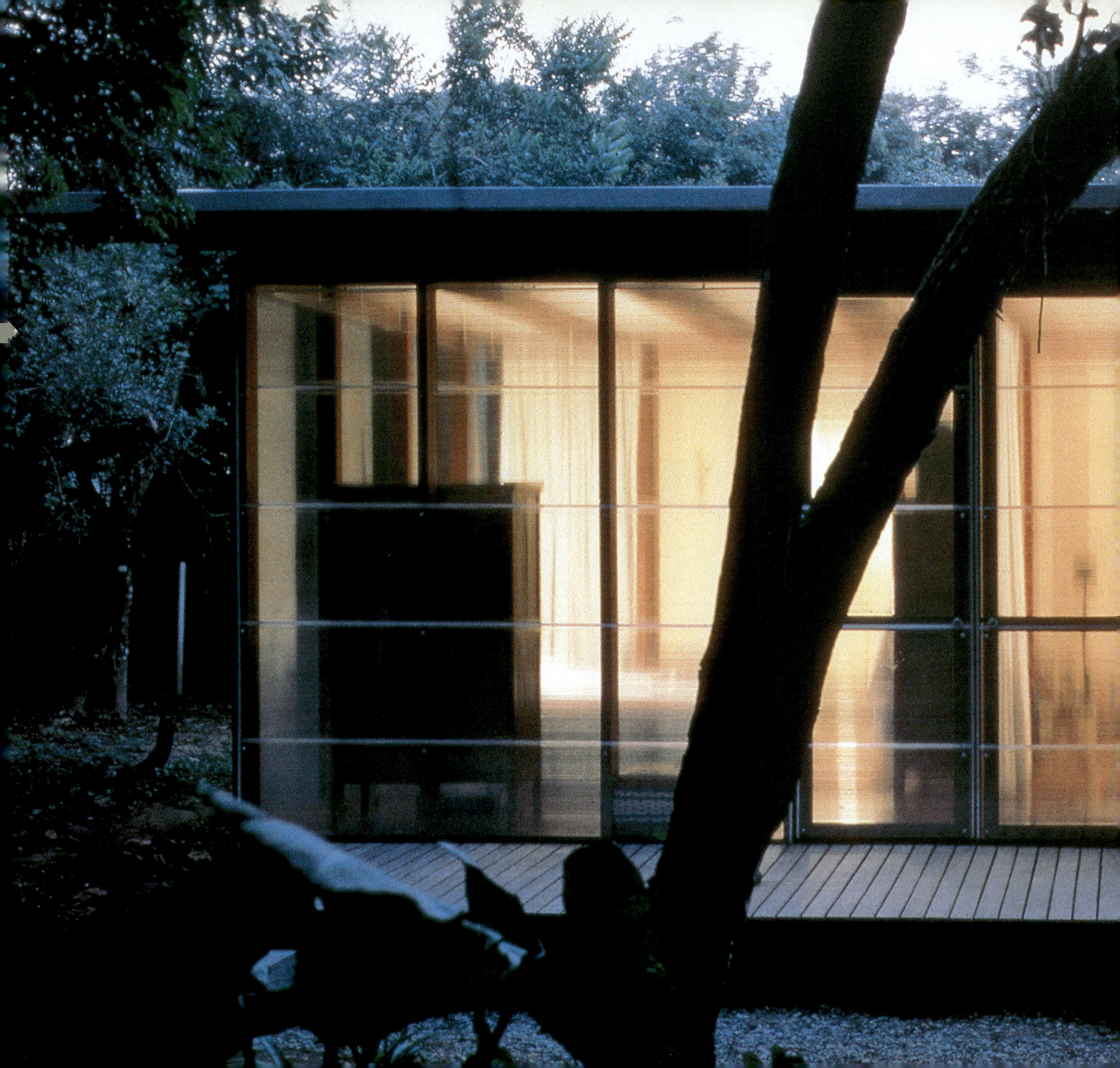

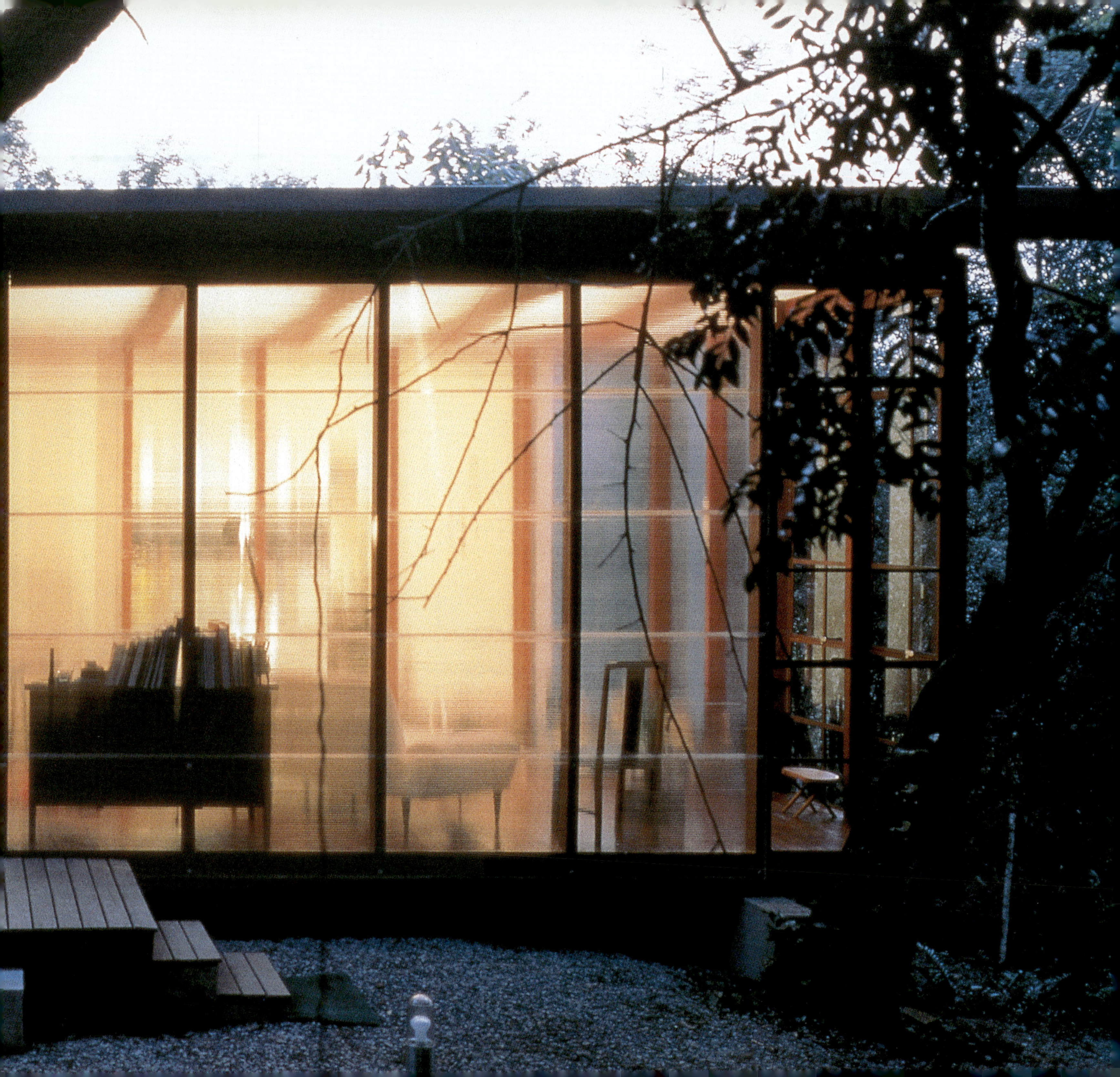

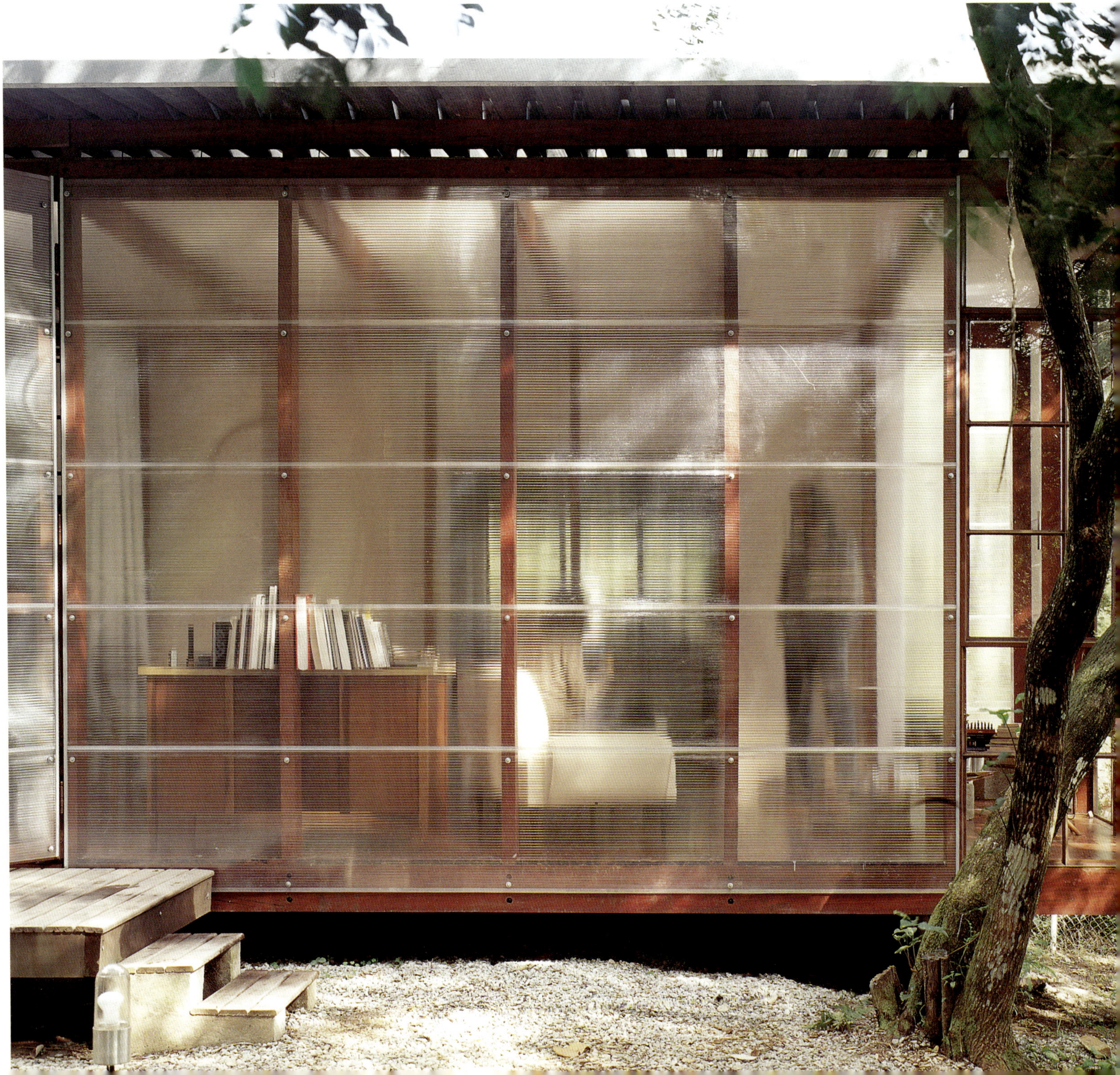

1 Social area in the north-east corner
2 View from the south

D'Alessandro House 117

House on the banks of the River Paraná
Arroyo Seco, Santa Fe, Argentina
1999

Rafael Iglesia

Client: *Meroi-Chaumet*
Photography: *Gustavo Frittegotto*

Placed against the powerful geography of the area surrounding the banks of the Paraná River, this small house of 70 sq.metres, a veritable refuge, incorporates a stimulating variety of spaces which reveal the shape of the territory through an architecture that is at one and the same time crude and refined. This refuge is built on a plot of land terraced on three levels and is open to the expansive horizon. It is run with surprising efficiency given its limited available resources.

Set on the edge of the gorge on the lower level of the terrain, close to the river and the jetty, the house becomes a place of contemplation sheltered from the aggressive winds. Because of this position the roof thus becomes part of the leisure areas around the swimming pool and, in this way, forms the reception space on the middle level. An expanse of water, filtered from the vast river, poeticises the landscape thereby appropriating the almost overwhelming presence of the territory and transforming it into a habitable place. The cascading water, which originates in the overflow from the swimming pool and is almost alongside you as you enter the house, interlaces the topographical planes in a sequence of direct but complex relatedness between the architecture and the site.

The structure of reinforced concrete and, in general, all tectonic decisions, are managed with an almost ascetic conciseness and with extreme severity. The inversion of the supporting beams to open the space to the views or protect the rear of the house from the heat of the evening sun, the subtle delimitation of form by planes of glass with no mullions on the corner, the natural eloquence of the pattern of stones in the floor, the challenging instability of the box built on the slope—all combine ably to construct minimum and powerful signs which clearly label and celebrate the site and its poignant mysteries.

1 Floor plan of access level
2 Floor plan of swimming pool level
3 Floor plan of house level
Opposite page: Partial view of the terrace and swimming pool

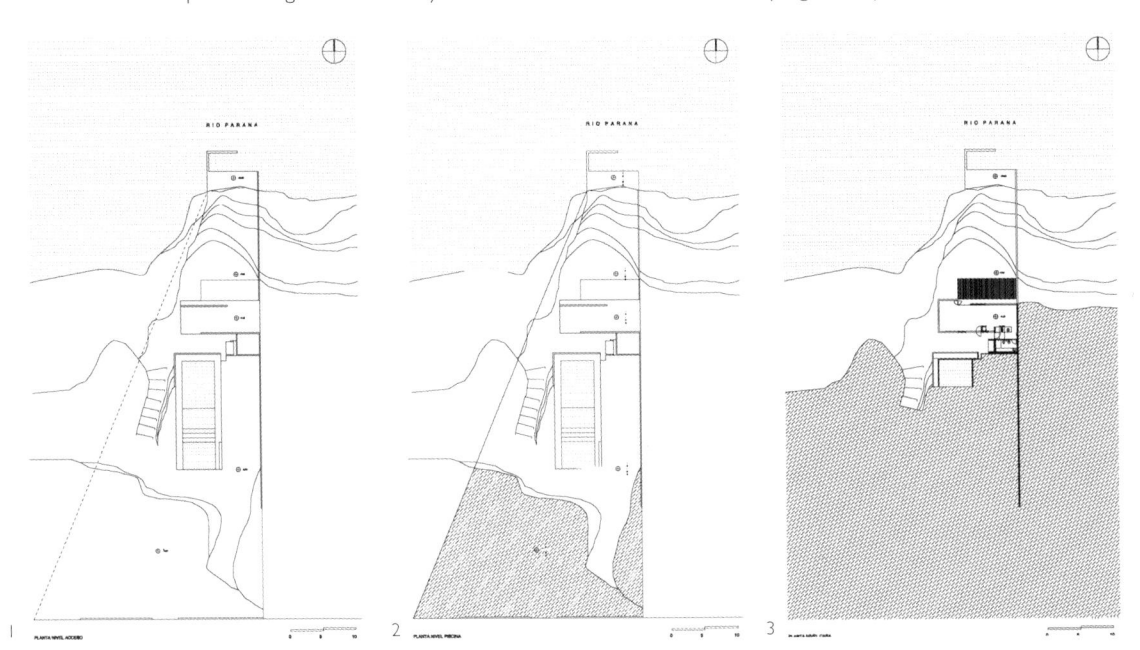

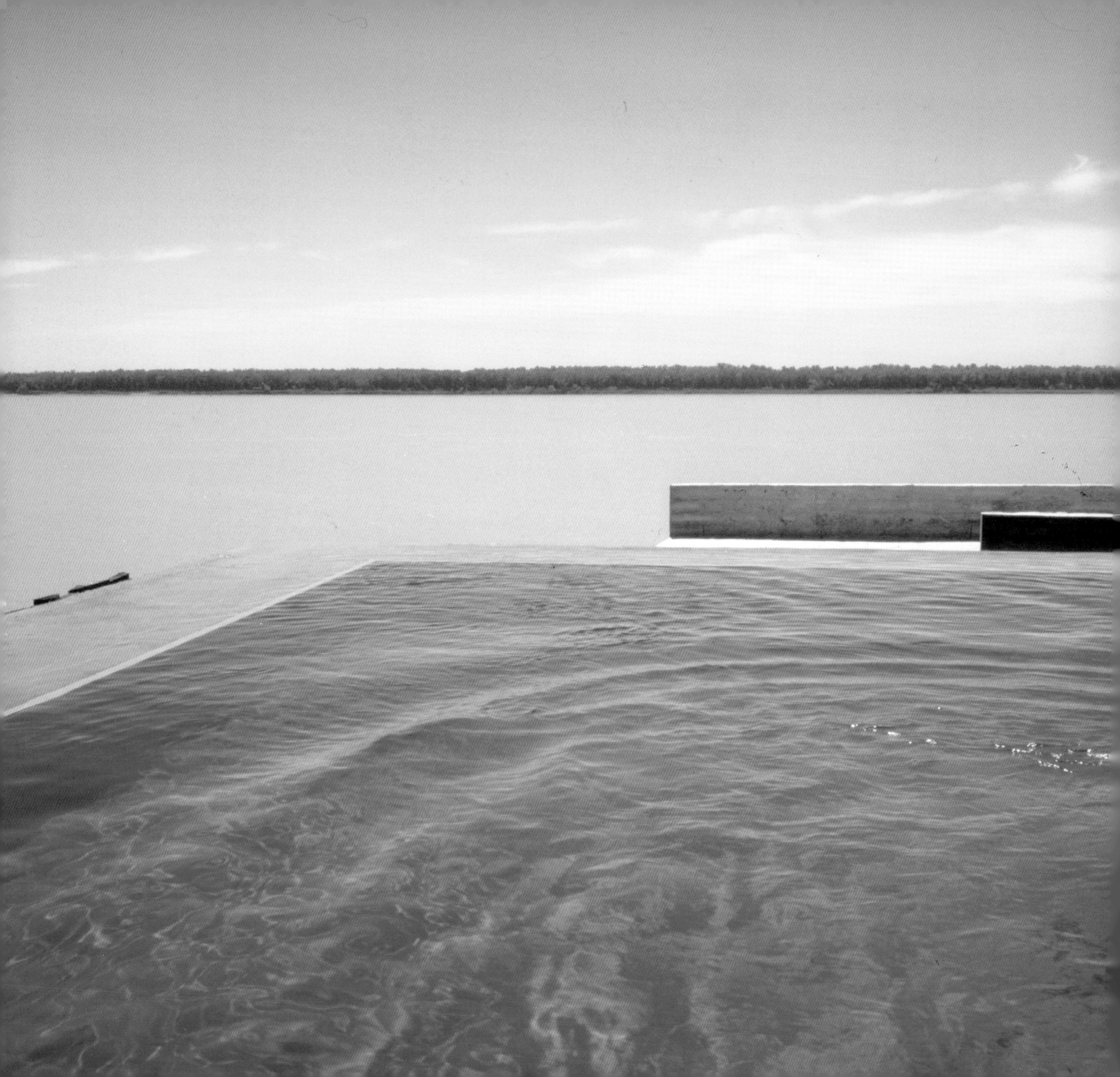

1 View from the banks
2 Section and façades
3 Partial view of the swimming pool

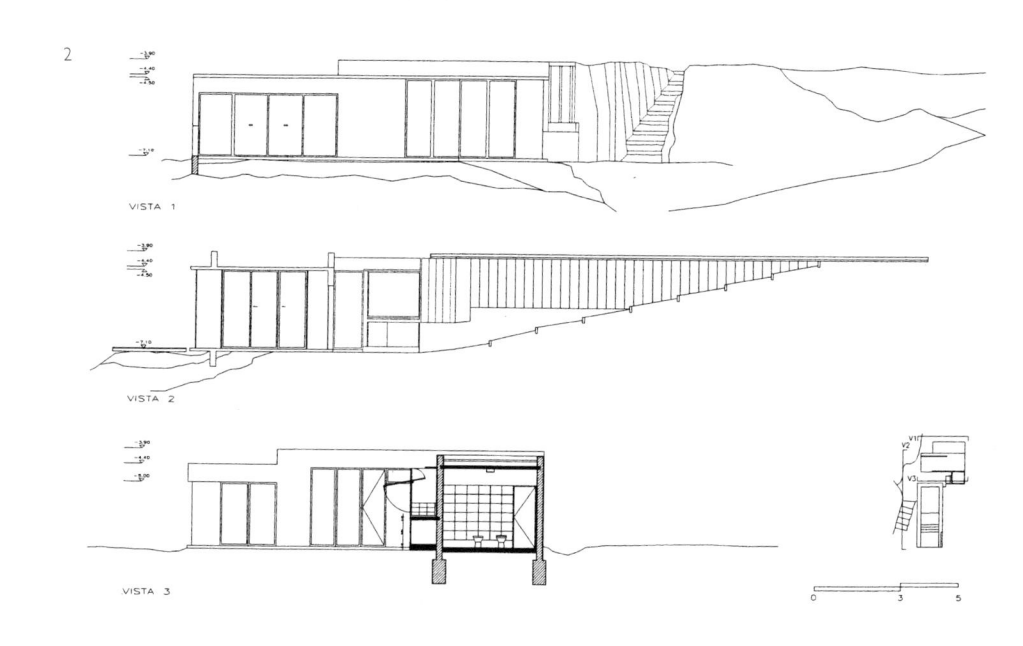

2

VISTA 1

VISTA 2

VISTA 3

0 3 5

1 Floor plan of house level
2 Longitudinal section
3 View towards the river
Opposite page: Access to the house

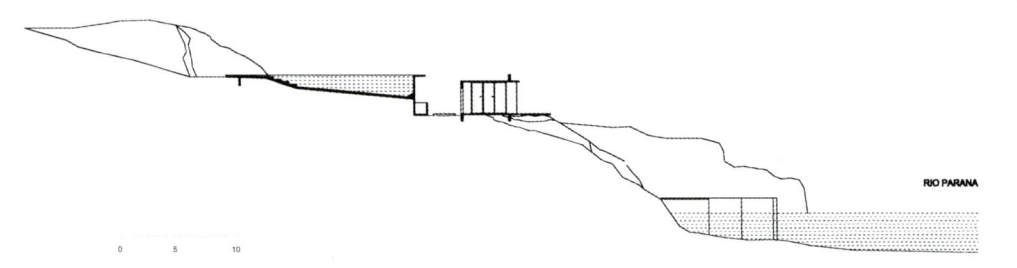

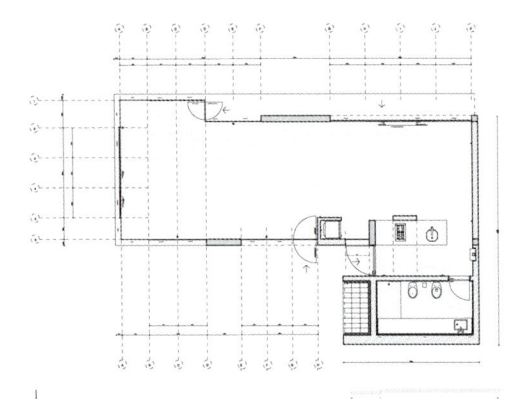

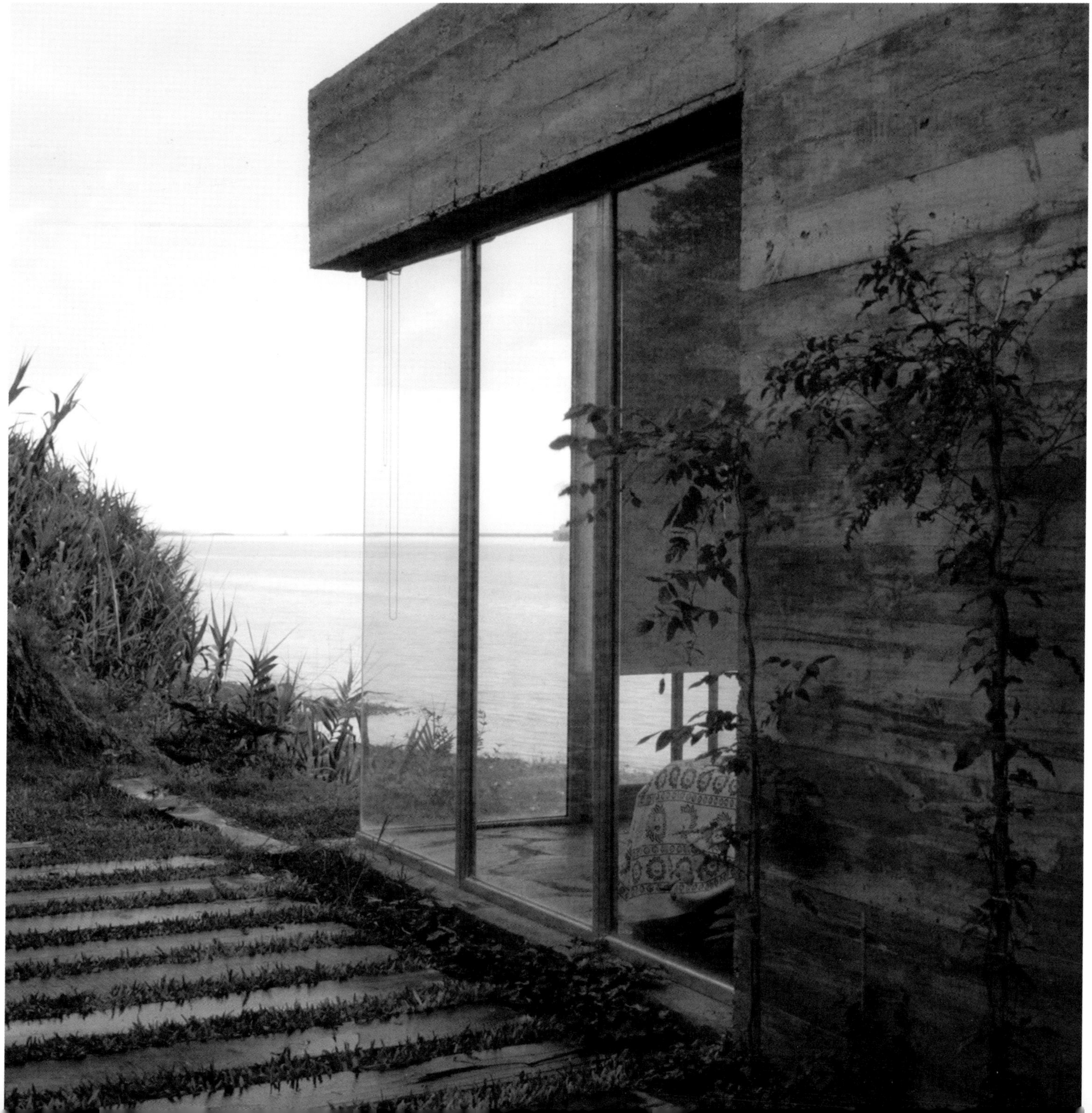

1   View towards the river
Opposite page: Access to the house

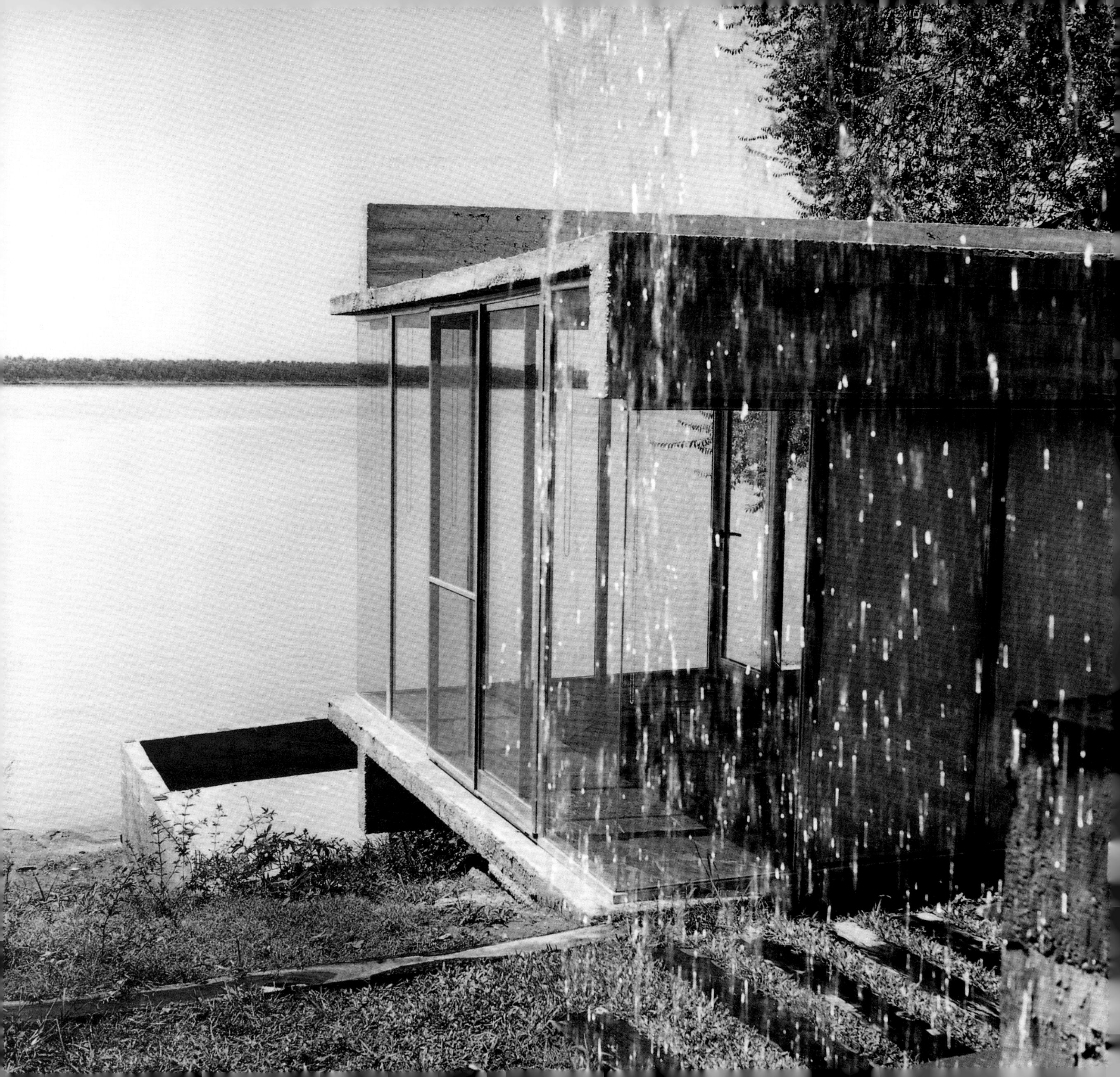

House at the Paulinia dam
Paulinia Dam, Municipality of Paulinia, Sao Paulo, Brazil
1992-1993

Renato Luiz Sobral Anelli

Client: *Nelson Rosa Jr.*
Master of works: *Aurelino Moreira*
Metallic structure: *High Tech (CV)*
Photography: *Tácito Carvalho e Silva*

The contrast between materials and structural forms, the overwhelming view towards the gentle downward slope of the terrain, the precise clarity of the structural lines and the freedom of unconventionality are the main architectural features of this holiday house on the shores of the lake created by the Paulinia dam, near to Sao Paulo.

On approach, the house appears as a solid block, formed by structural brick walls, the only opening being the entrance. This volume, which contains the spaces for the service areas and an equally solid basement which houses the bedrooms, provides the space in which the social activities of the house take place. It gives unobstructed views of the distant scene and seems almost to be an independent building sited on the alternative territory created by the brick volume.

The architecture of this place, little more than a fragile shack sustained physically and functionally by the mass forming the plinth which supports it, evolves from the lightness of the steel structure covered by a white luminous roof made of corrugated heat-and-sound-proofed metal sheets with a PVC finish. The spaces are so arranged that they keep out direct sunlight in the summer while providing the maximum in winter.

The glass wall, which provides maximum contrast to the opaque steel structure, is formed by transparent and continuous planes that allow the unobstructed flow of the interior towards the expansive exterior and thus subtly outlining the horizon. The fragile roof and plain walls define the area set aside for social activities, moving in the direction of the terrace and swimming pool in a sequence of descending planes which end at ground level.

1 Isometric projection. View from the dam
Opposite page: Central area of the swimming pool

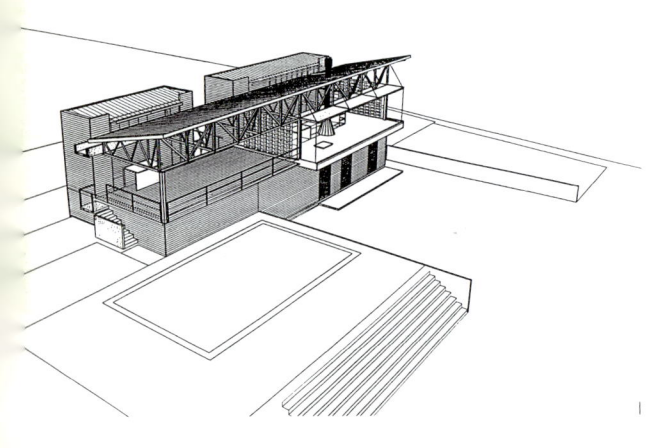

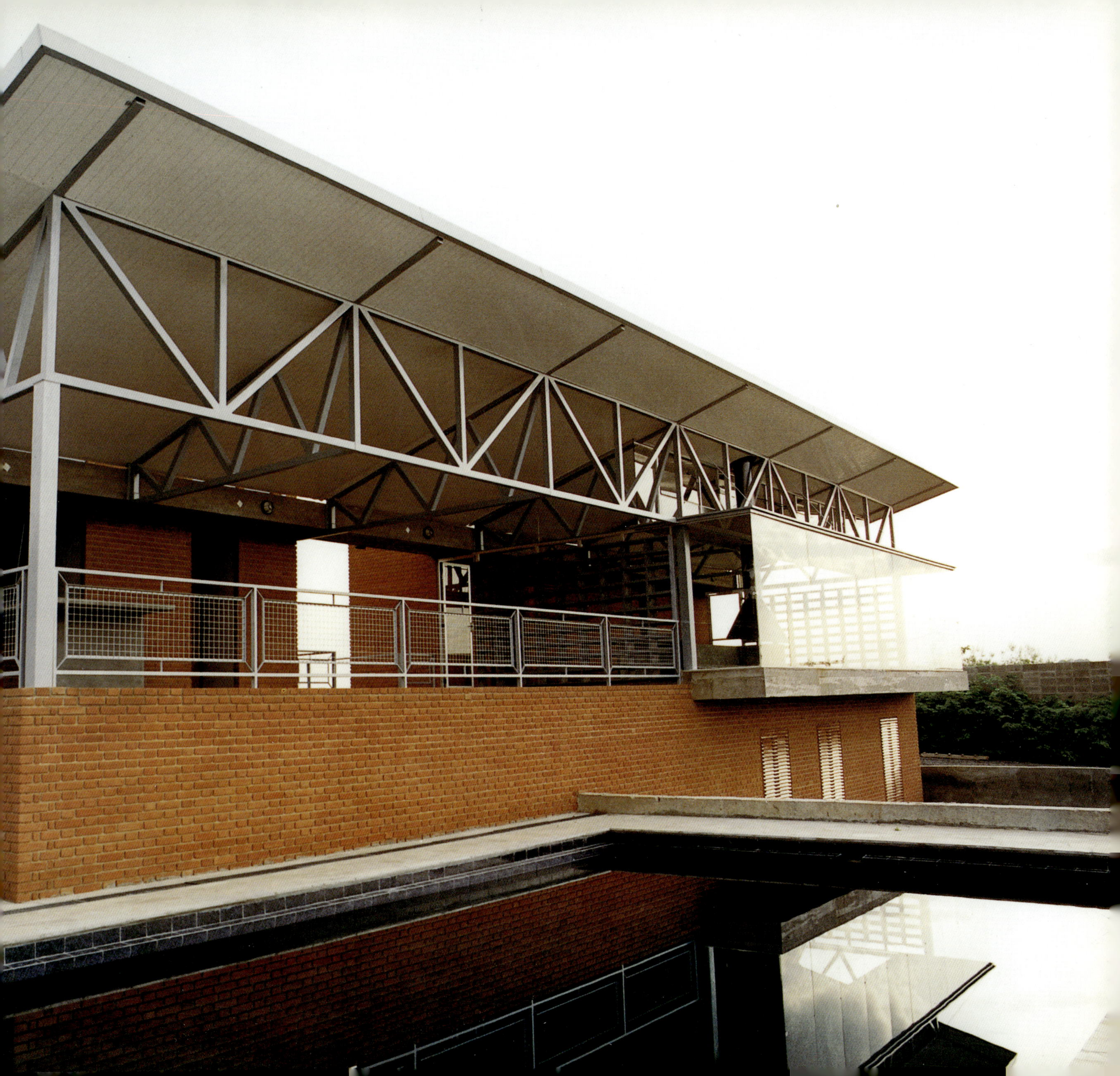

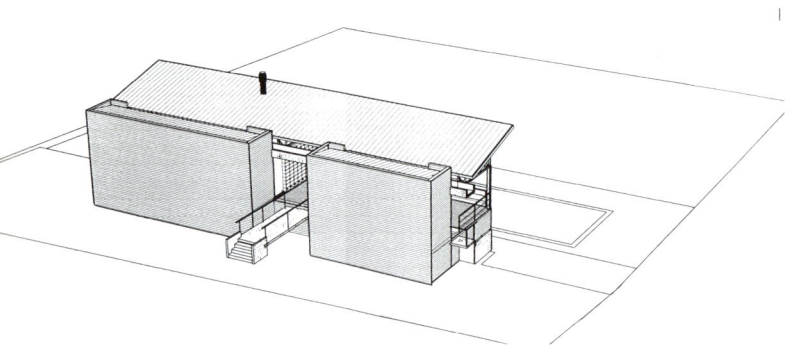

1 Isometric projection. View from the access
2 View from the east
3 Floor plan of the access level and the rooms
4 View from the north

1. Access
2. Terrace
3. Access to the swimming pool
4. Barbecue
5. Bathroom
6. Living room
7. Engine room
8. Stairs
9. Kitchen
10. Bedrooms

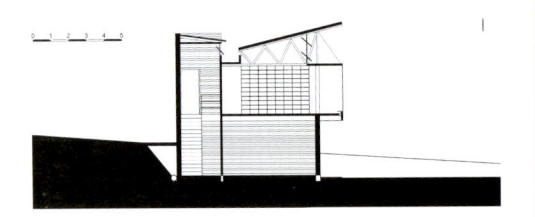

1   Cross section
Large photo: Main area

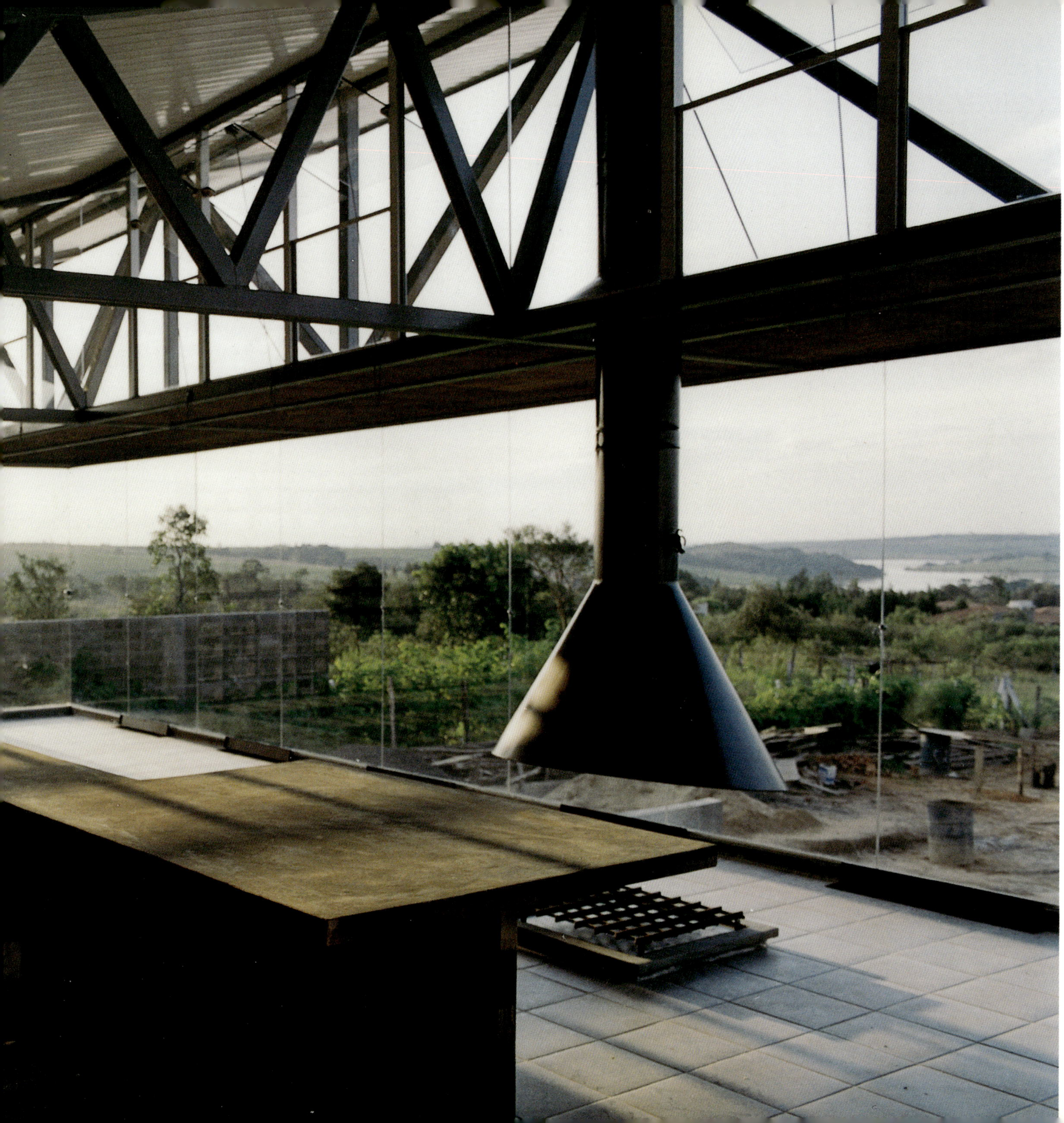

Posada House

El Retiro, Antioquia, Colombia
1994-1995

Echeverri Arquitectos

Architects: *Alejandro Echeverri R. / Juan Bernardo Echeverri C.*
Architecture: *Echeverri Arquitectos / Alejandro Echeverri R.. / Juan Bernardo Echeverri C. / Luis Fernando Morales / Ligia Fernández*
Structures: *Luis Bernardo González*
Electrical installations: *Juan Gonzalo Ríos*
Sanitary installations: *Ricardo Aguilar*
Construction: *Luis Fernando Tobon*
Photography: *Alejandro Echeverri R.*

The house set atop a hillside that slopes down towards a pine forest, is in a rural area close to the city of Medellín. The two wings, which house the domestic activities, form an angle that suggests the typical patio of a large country house, though in this case incomplete, delimited by the profile of the topography and open to the wide landscape which thus completes in the distance the site of an architecture expanding outwards.

The exterior surfaces of the house, built as brick walls on a plinth of green stone, seem solid and almost impassable. The measured perforations give little clue to the systematic arrangement of the family rooms, while a high window, linking the wall with the sloping plane of the roof, illuminates the interior through the reflection of the light on the structure of the ceiling; a doorway in the corner provides access. The surfaces, composed on the basis of the transparency of the materials of which they are made, make the ensemble seem somewhat enormous. This, contrasted with the imposing character of the landscape and the eloquence of the natural presences, establishes a delicate balance of forms, scales and textures.

Towards the patio, a series of transparent sliding windows beneath wide eaves, which brings to mind the depth of traditional corridors, gives an air of continuity to the rooms leading to the green patio and, through it, towards the distant views.

A covered terrace, which crowns the social activities area, is astutely moulded to close the circuit around the patio while giving continuity to the views in the axial direction of the body to which it belongs; it also contains the main living room and provides an area for informal activities. At the end of the body of rooms, an open platform extends the main bedroom out over the welcoming density of the landscape of pines.

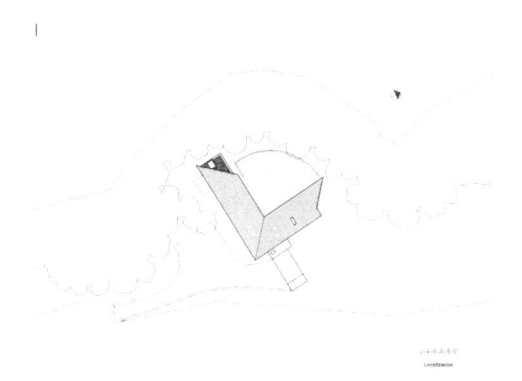

1 Site plan
2 Section through the patio
Opposite page: Terrace of the main room

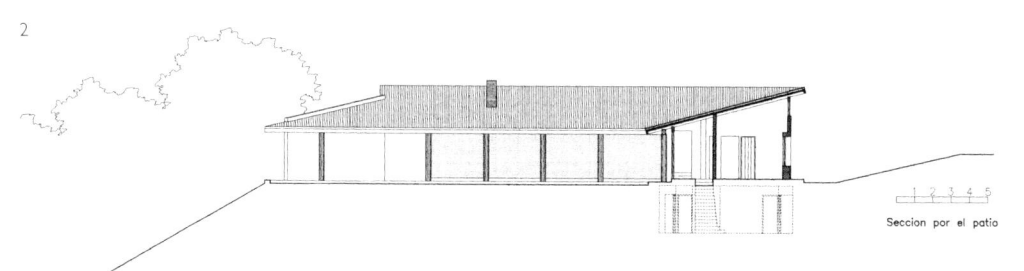

Posada House 133

1 Floor plan
2 Access façade elevation
Large photo: Main access

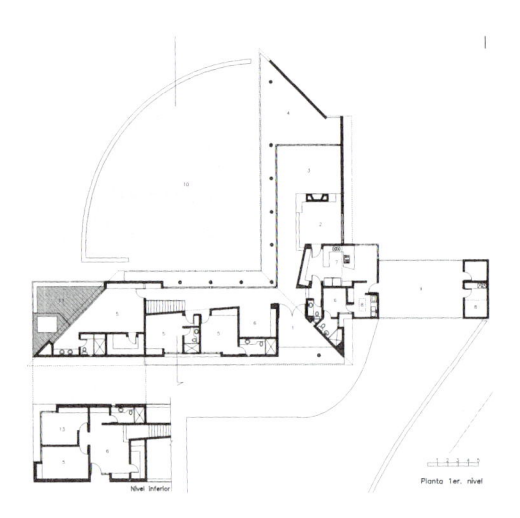

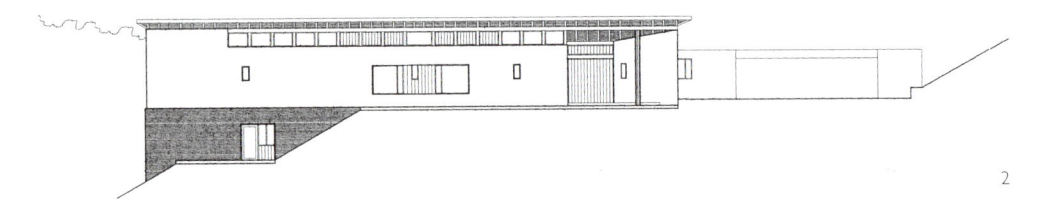

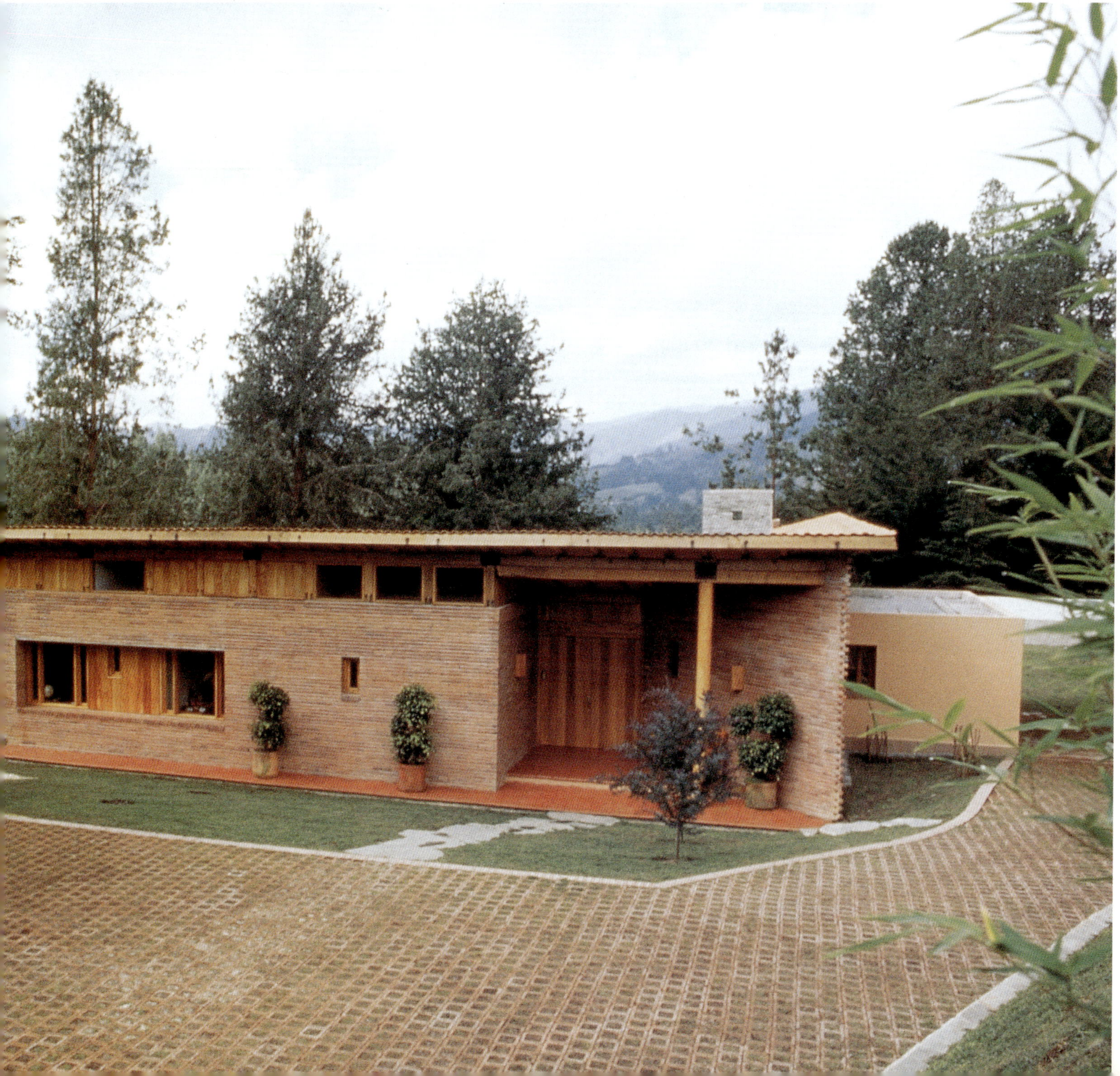

1   View of the ensemble
2   Living room terrace
Opposite page: View of the garden from the living room

136

Posada House 137

Amsterdam House

Mexico City, Mexico
1996-1998

Teodoro González de León

Collaborator: *Miguel Barbachano Osorio*
Structural design: *Diseño y Supervisión, S.C. "DYS"*
Electrical installations: *COESA Ingeniería, S.A.*
Hydraulic and sanitary installations: *Garza Maldonado y Asociados, S.C.*
Builder: *Engineer Miguel Cornejo*
Photography: *Pedro Hiriart / Luis Gordoa*

1 Roof plan

Large photo: View of the patio from the main living room

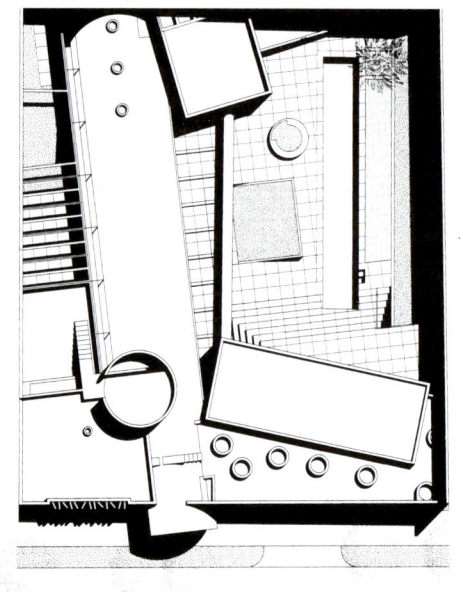

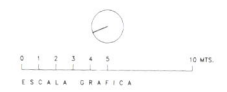

Located in the central Colonia Hipódromo Condesa, in Mexico City, on an plot of land which is almost square and which is lower than the surrounding terrain, the house evolves upon a platform raised 1.2m above street level and around the patio which is created by the complex connections between its volumes.

Each component of the programme takes on a different form: a barrel vault houses the hall, the living room and the library; a cube the painting workshop; a rectangular prism, set atop a platform of steps which hides the garage houses the bedrooms; while a cylinder converging on the vault contains the service areas.

This is a careful assembly of differing volumes, rotated slightly to enhance the views of the spaces above the patio, shaping a territory in its own right from the multiple evocations which they suggest, from the powerful formal presence of the relationships which they establish and from the renewed visions with which the changes in the light give shape to the territory.

Looking like a collection of objects found by chance and arranged spontaneously, these volumes are freely placed and, as if dealing with the accidental remains of an excavation, transform the surface which supports them into an architectural landscape that is physically autonomous and closed, though full of echoes and allusions to the past.

The contrasts and even ambiguities arising from the interaction between these diverse forms are interspersed with the thrustful continuity of the white concrete surfaces and the stone floors which dissolve the opposing space between the rooms and the patio. The shapes projected by the dramatic effects of the light on the textured surfaces emphasise the sensorial harmony of these spaces of ancestral contemporaneity.

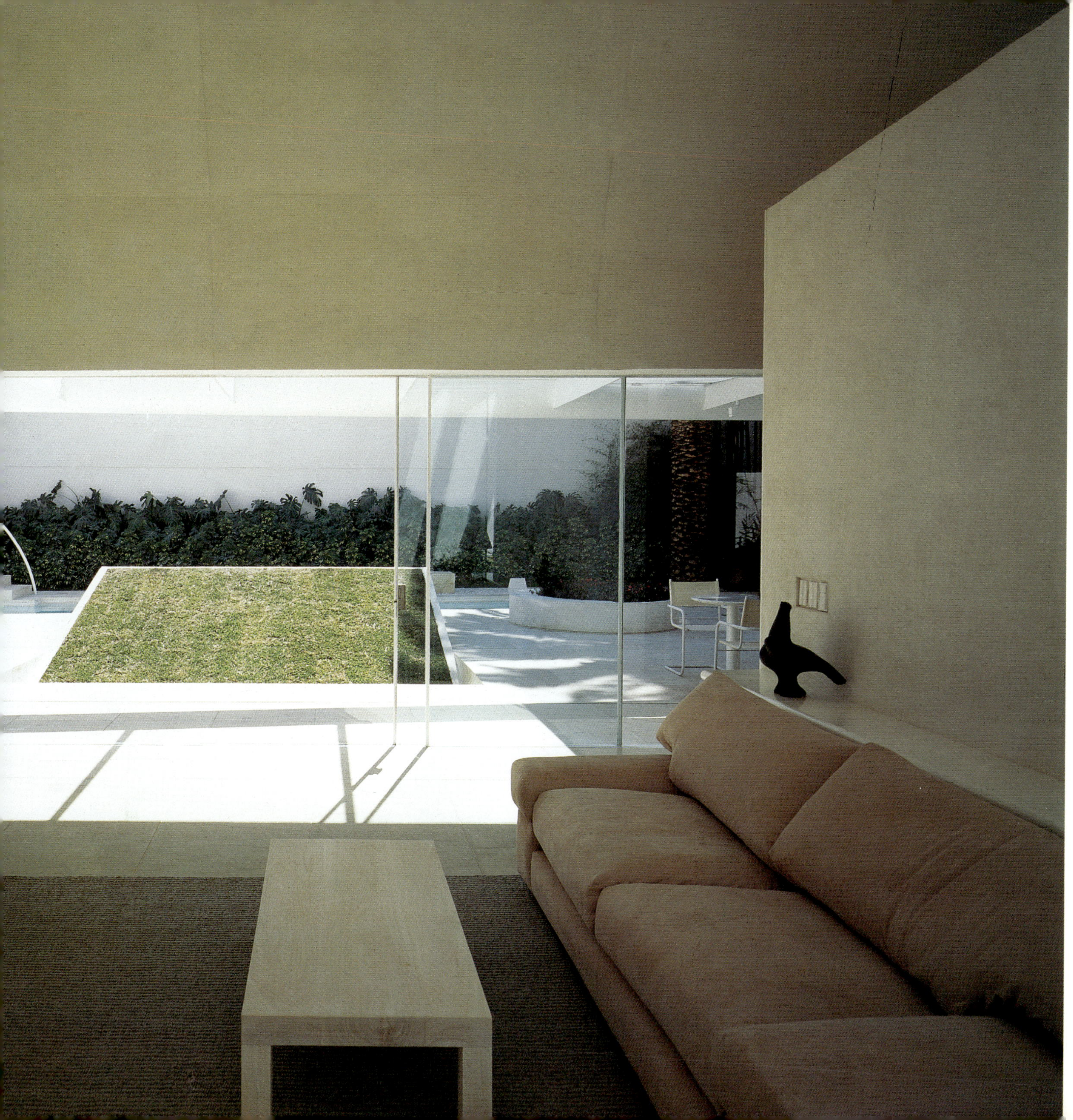

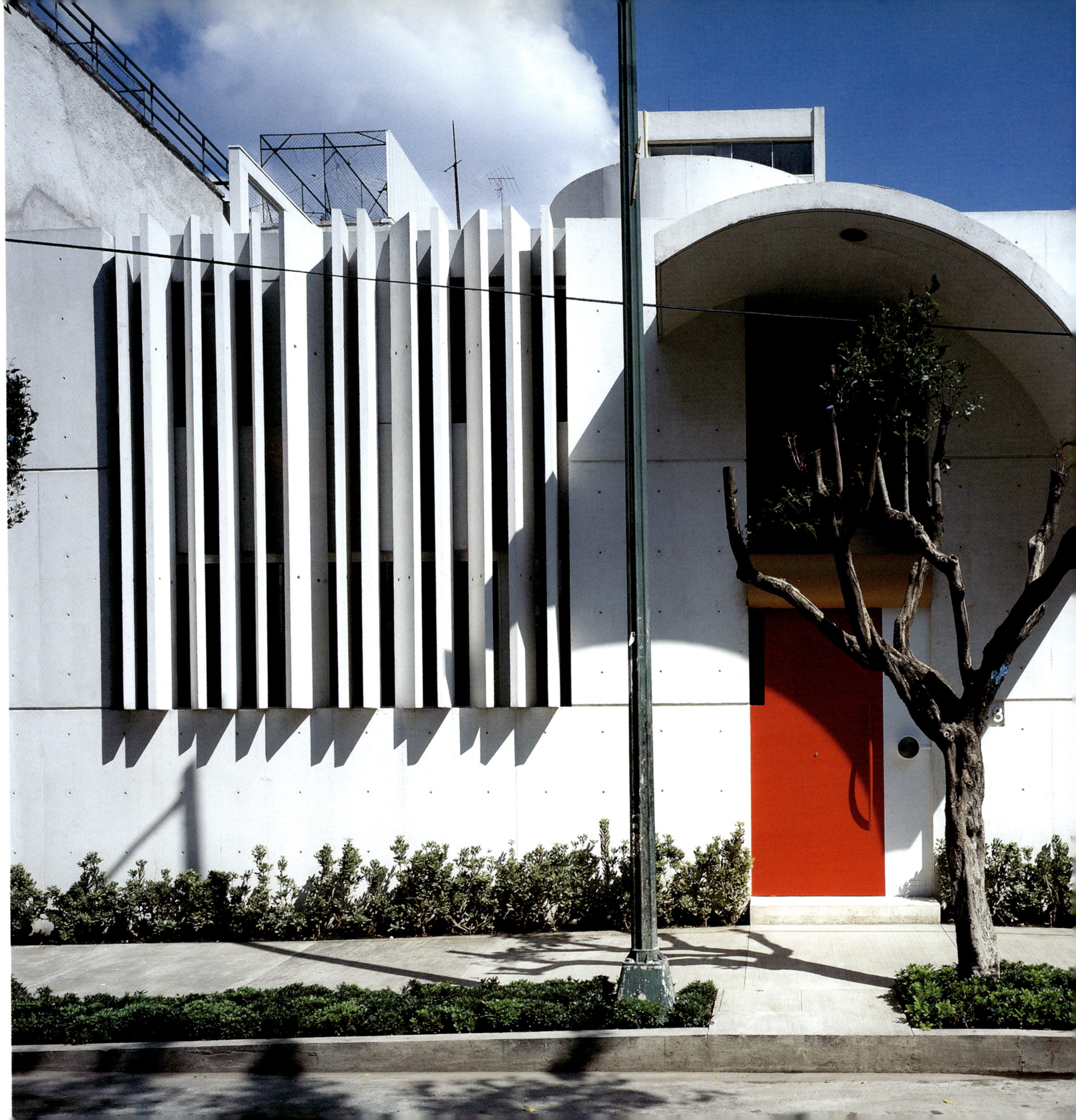

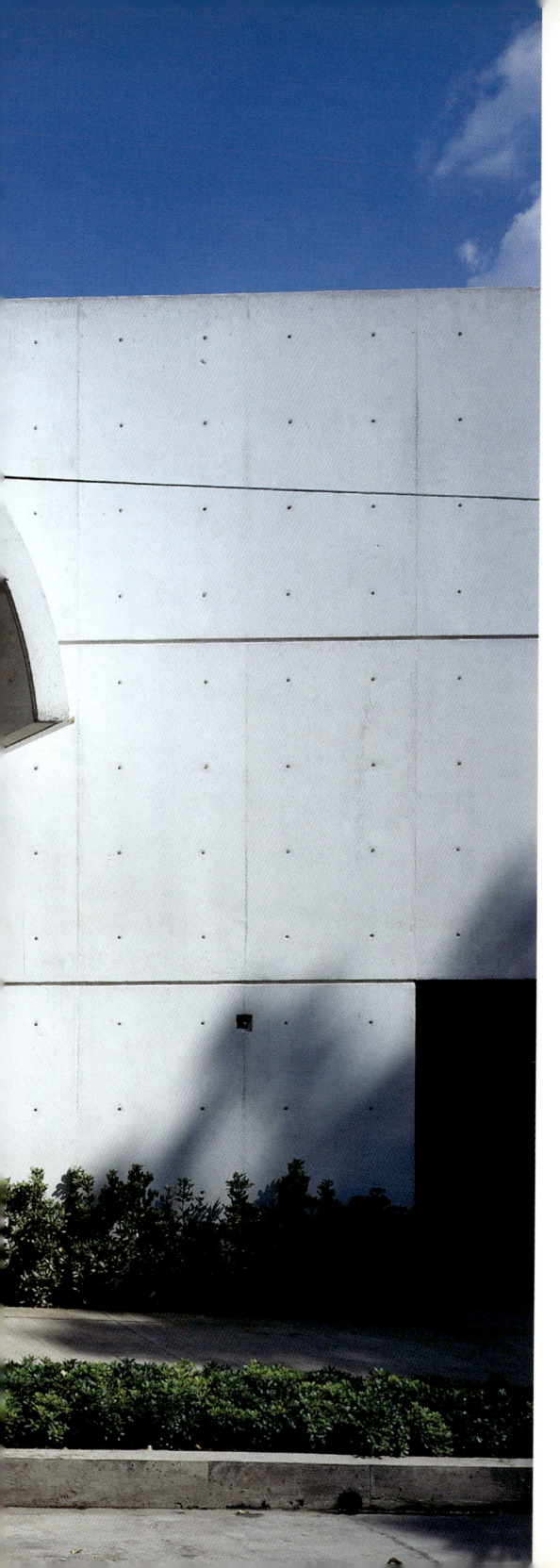

Full page: Access façade
1 and 2 Sections

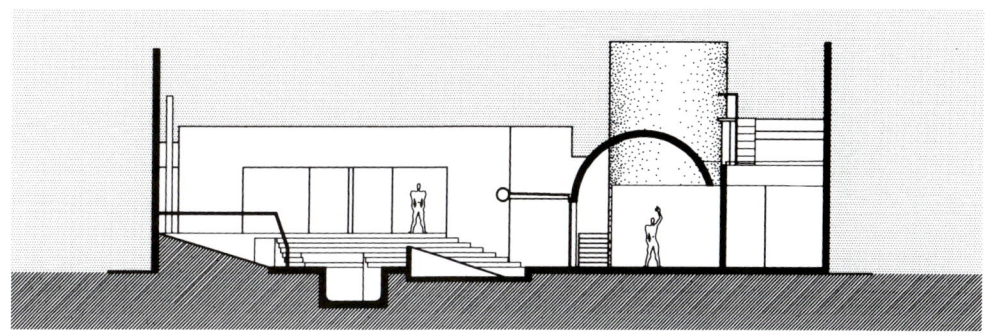

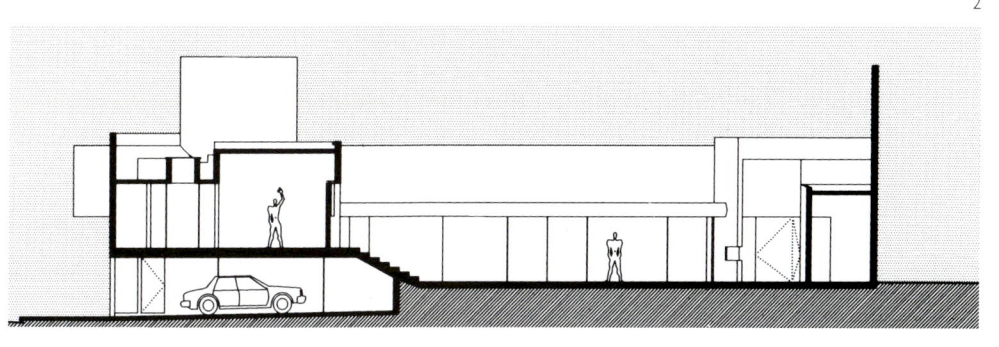

Amsterdam House

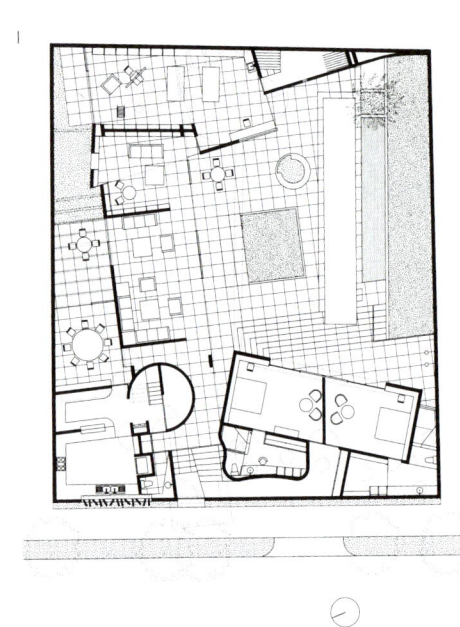

1 Floor plan
2 View of the access from the living room
Opposite page: View of the study from the living room

Amsterdam House 143

1 View of the volume housing the bedrooms
2 Study
3 Perspective of the patio from the study

3

La Ribereña

Caracas, Venezuela
1977-1985

Jimmy Alcock

Client: *Isabel Lecuna / Gustavo y Patricia Cisneros*
Architecture: *Jimmy Alcock / Frank Alcock / Luis F. Barón / R. Colevecchio*
Landscaping: *Roberto Burle Marx*
Floor mural: *Nedo M. F.*
Isometric projections: *Gaetano Zapulla, for* Espacio magazine, Sociedad Editora Latinoamericana C. A.
Photography: *Paolo Gasparini*

A group of shapes, arranged on the gentle downward slope of the terrain, form a kind of citadel confined by a plain solid wall over the street and a gorge to the south.

The two axes around which the composition is arranged permit the identification of the hierarchies and relatedness between the parts. To walk through them is to gain first-hand knowledge of an open and permeable layout which merges with the luxuriant natural environment, revealed in the interstices, distances and spaces between forms. To the permeability of volume and space is added the wealth of texture of the brick walls that celebrate the intense tropical light by introducing a precise but at the same time ambiguous limit which seems to dissolve the borders of the house, leaving them open to an expansive play of reversible spatial cycles.

Access to the house evolves from a kind of sluice in which the door is set, and proceeds along a corridor as deep as a hallway and as luminous as a gallery, to a vestibule which connects the main living room and the dining room and leads to the garden and the swimming pool. Thus, the interior becomes a continuous unit with the outside, in much the same way as the exterior view of the built-up landscape, in its many outlets, announces that the interior frames the appropriated natural environment of which it forms a part.

The space for everyday activities is arranged in two clearly differentiated blocks. To the east, two interlaced walls house the living room, in a form which is compact yet open, and which links the patio (designed by Roberto Burle Marx) to the main garden. To the west, an almost capricious grouping of shapes houses the bedrooms and generates patios and gardens. Between them, a horizontal plane which covers the dining room and receives the access, modulates the continuity of the territory while framing the criss-cross views which define the house as a continuum of spaces and experiences.

1 Sketch
Opposite page: Main access

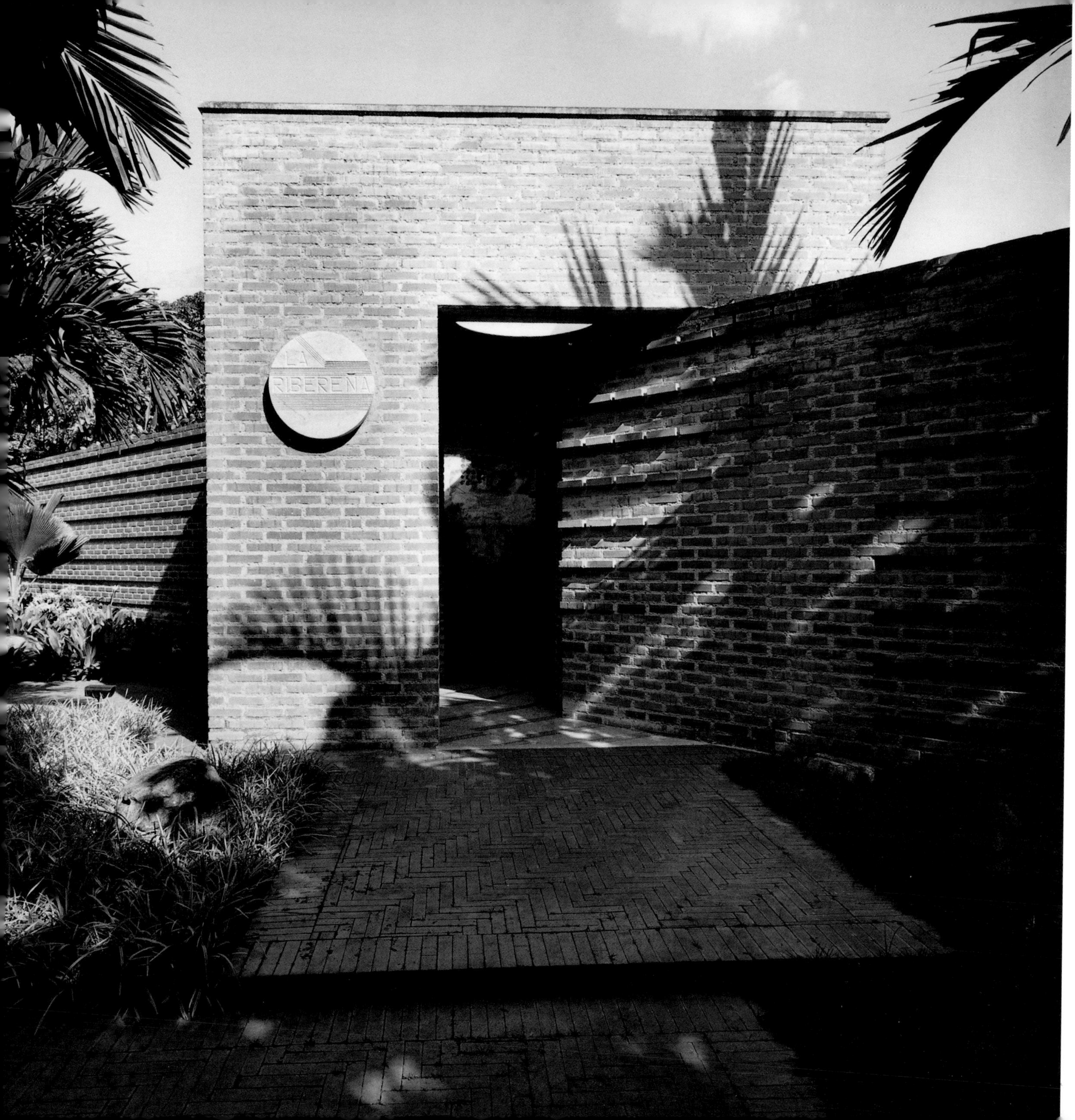
LA
RIBEREÑA

1 Interior view of the main access
2 Access corridor
3 and 4 Sections
5 Façade towards the garden

La Ribereña 149

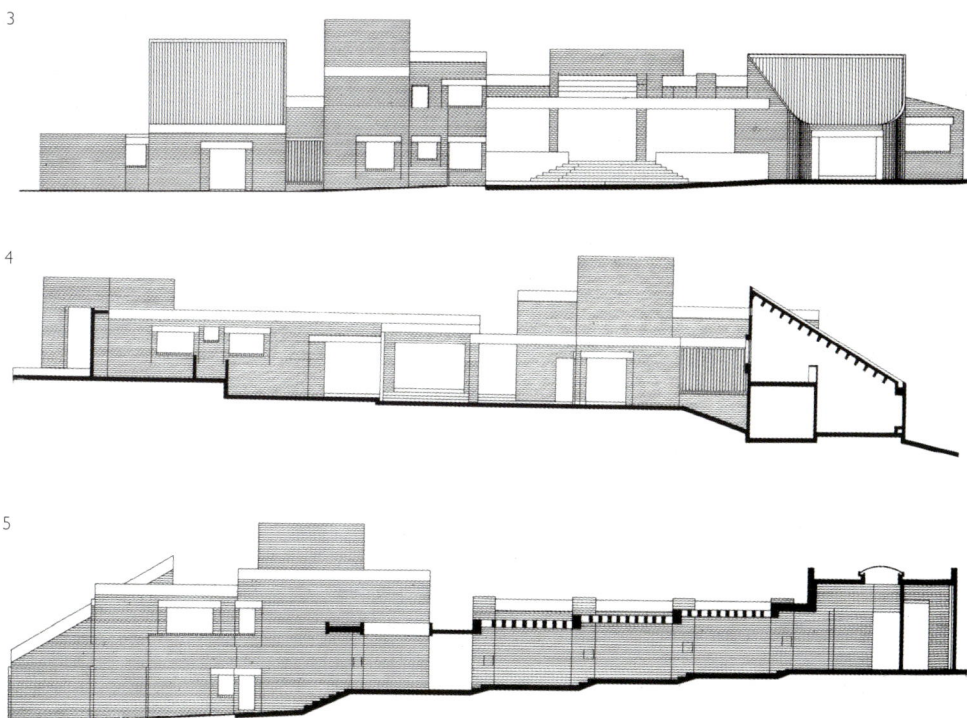

1 Isometric projection. Spatial structure
2 Isometric projection. Volumetric structure
Large photo: View from the swimming pool

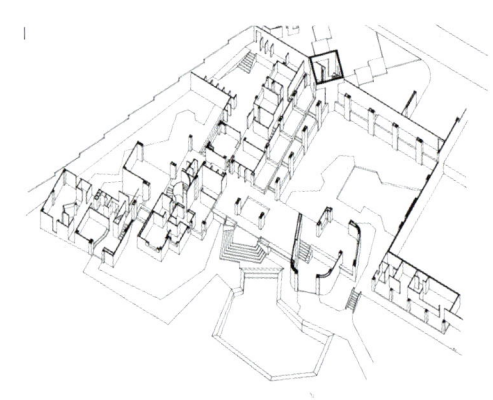

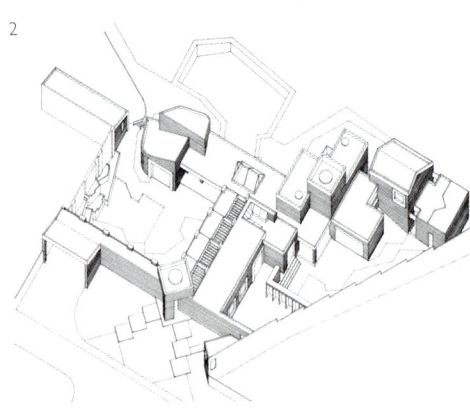

La Ribereña   151

1 Floor plan
2 Access corridor
Opposite page: Entrance to the bedrooms area

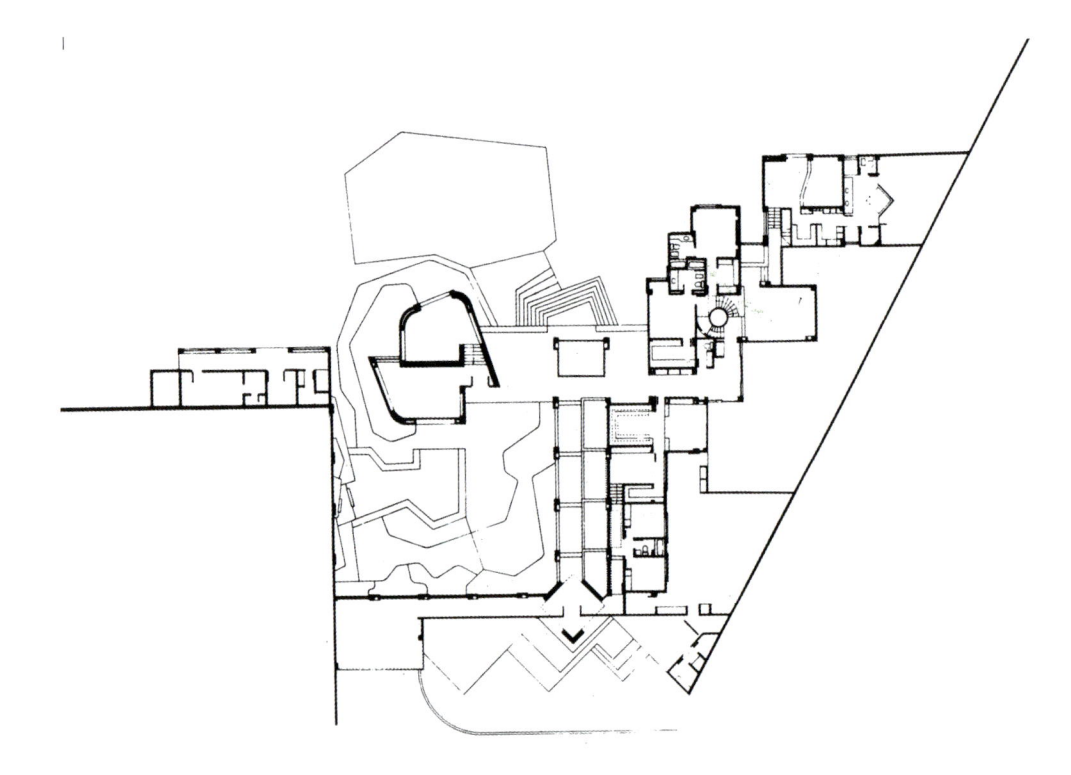

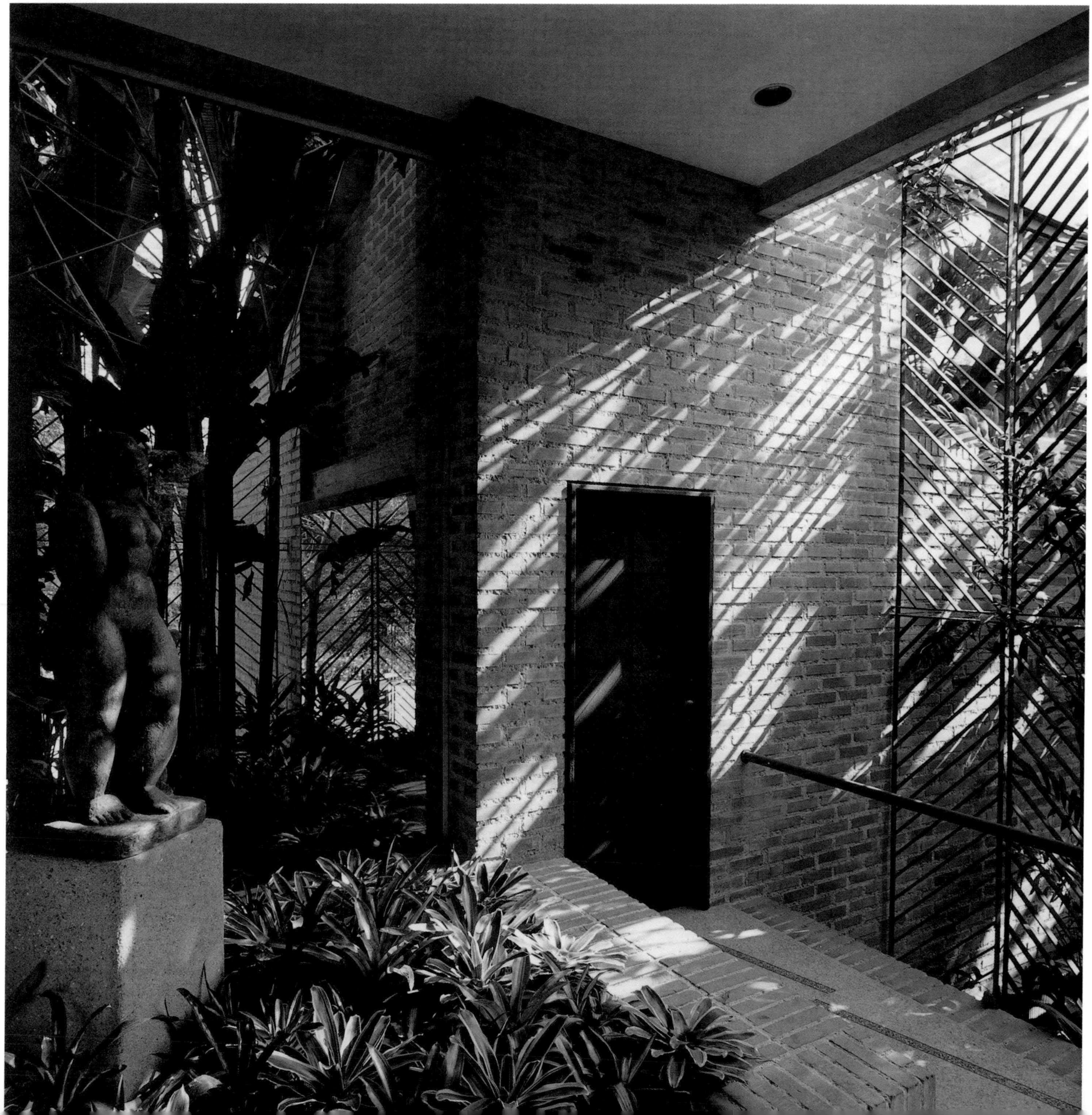

La Reina House
Fundo Totoralillo, Los Vilos, Chile
1995-1996

Cristian Boza / J. Lührs / F. Muzard

Client: *The Boza-Wilson family*
Photography: *Guy Wenborne*

Built to the specifications of a 3m x 3m modular pattern on a large territory with unobstructed view of the Andes mountain range, this house forms a bridge across what was formerly a gorge. It was designed by the architect for himself as a "product of the personal interaction with my wife, who is not an architect, and with my children".

Its architectural development incorporates the traditional "parrones"—galleries hung with vines and used in popular Chilean architecture as a means of protection against the climate—into transparently modern spaces, submerged in the landscape as the sphere of the domestic life.

The rhythmic wooden supports define a framework of places which intensify the views over the mountain range and the smaller individual landscapes belonging to the house itself. The suggestion of a patio, the anchoring of the bridge with a block of stones, the solid glazed or semi-glazed walls, the uninterrupted articulation of the spaces and of the interior to the exterior through the intervention of the *parrones*, the sculptural force of a silk-cotton tree, a group of palms or an ombú tree and the vertical emphasis of a turret—all are used as signs of habitation in a territory which was conceived as a unit, thereby emphasising the sensory over the visual, the general over the specific and the experience of the space over the recognition of the forms.

Access beneath the main structure is by a stairway leading to a terrace which is open to the mountain range to the north-east. In the interior, a limited palette of natural materials alternates to denote the different scales and hierarchies within the uniform pattern of the constructive building module.

In the garden, walls and terraces of locally quarried stone interweave, with a certain naturalistic nonchalance, the experience of the central construction with the presence of the mountain landscape arranging the vegetable species and the ornamental elements to avoid individual prominence.

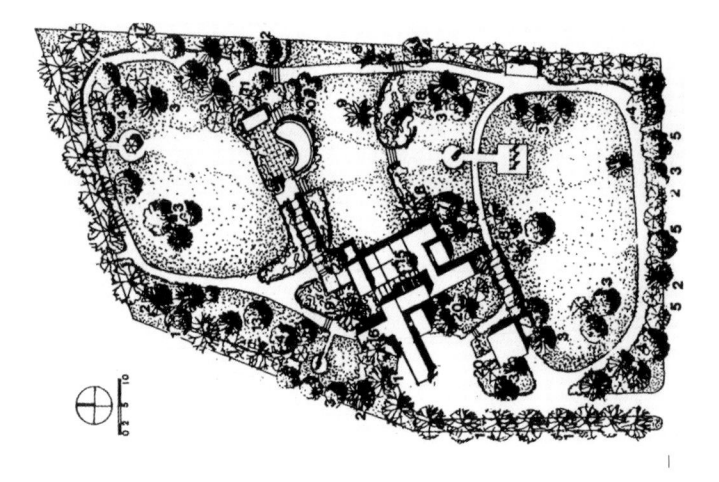

1 Site plan
Opposite page: Terrace giving access to the house

La Reina House 155

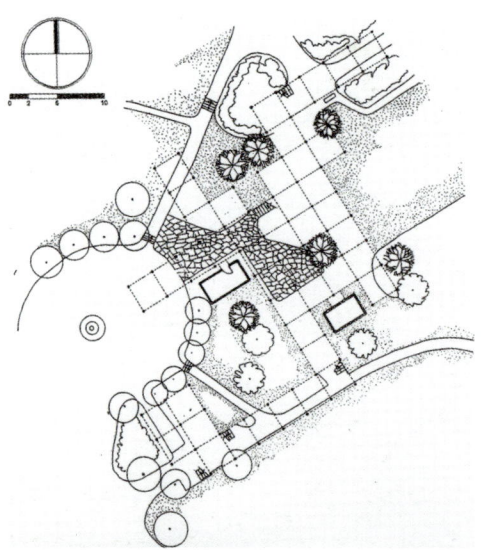

1 Floor plan of the lower level
2 Detail of the union of the access level with the terrace
3 Floor plan of the first level
4 Detail of the main access stairway

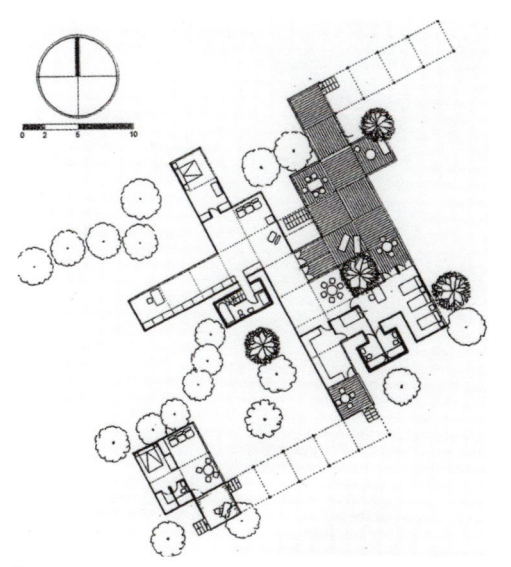

3

4

1   Section, towards the mountain range
2   Section, from the mountain range
3   Library
Large photo: Dining room

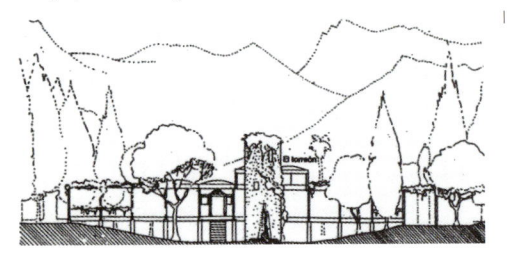

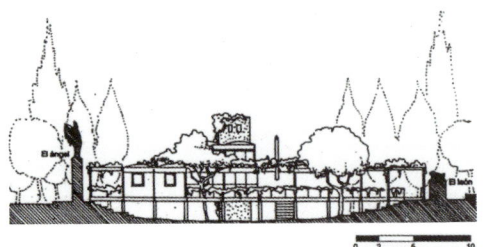

158

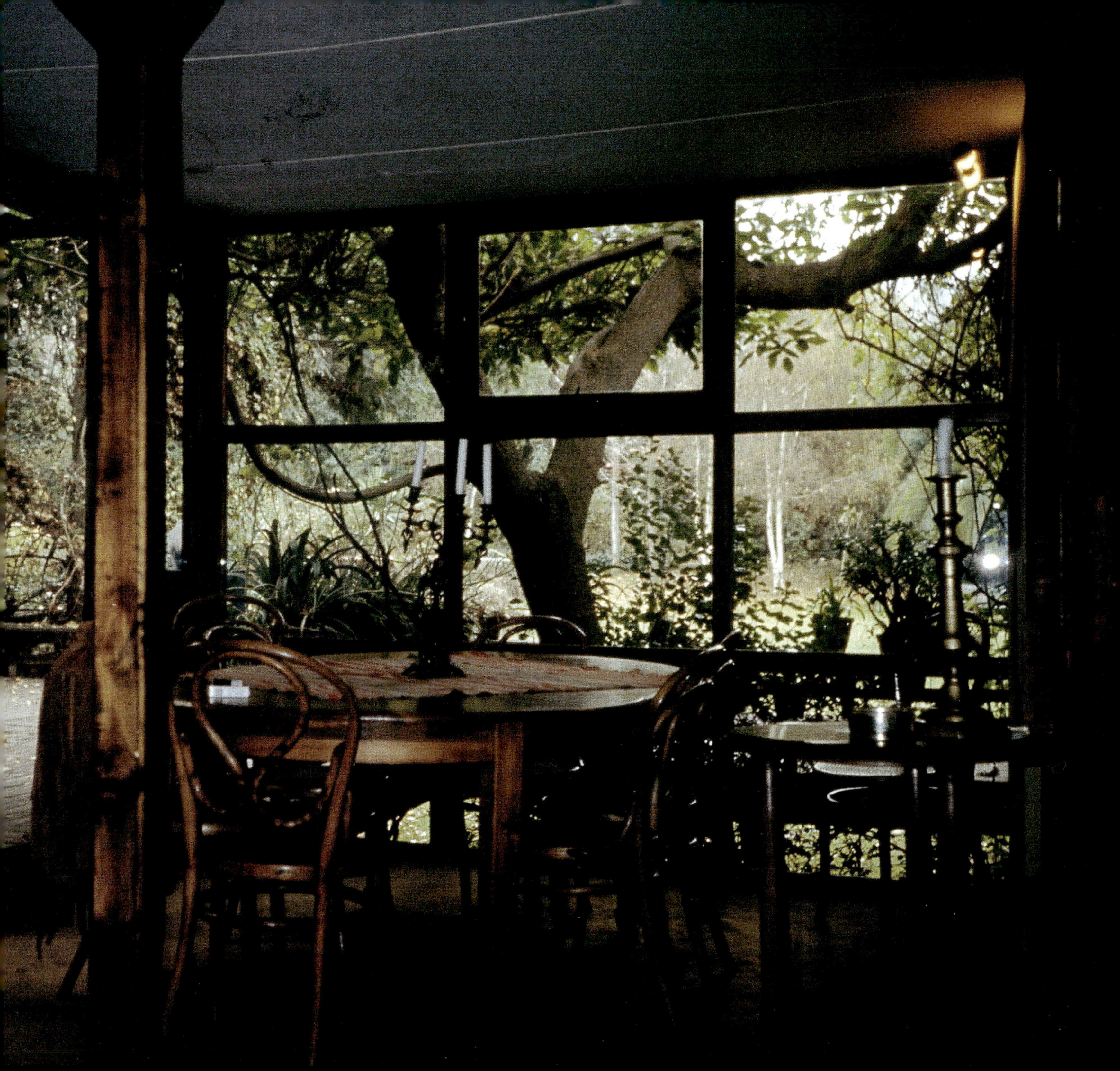

Negro House

Contadero, Mexico State, Mexico
1995-1997

Alberto Kalach

Collaborators: *Gustavo Lipkau / Rosa López*
Structural design: *Guillermo Tena*
Ironwork: *Jorge Segura*
Landscaping: *Tonatiuth Martínez*
Construction: *Daniel Álvarez Fernández*
Photography: *Luis Gordoa / Paul Czitrom / Martha Irene Alcántara*

East of Mexico City, on a steep hillside which descends between holm oaks and tepozan trees towards a ravine, are four habitable structures which seem to be floating in the landscape like long platforms atop the more gentle topography of existing paths, in a dynamic cadence of tense relatedness. The platforms are grafted onto the terrain like bridges whose limited supports avoid the use of containing walls which would affect the roots of the nearby trees. The foundations also generate a system of cisterns for storing the rain water running down from the roofs and patios. In this way, the structures organise the spaces of the house while respecting topography, vegetation and orientations. Each structure preserves the rhythms and proportions appropriate to its function, character and scale. The inflections between the bodies and the continuing articulation of the spaces in each of them with the interstices generated by their interrelationship with the others produce an ambiguous flow between the interior and the exterior and create space which constructs the territory as a continuity between what is built and what is natural.

With the clarity of a discernible geometrical system, concrete, steel, wood and glass are assembled in modules which manifest the unity between space, form and structure. The contrasts between transparency and opacity transform the neutrality of the enclosing surfaces in an orderly and complex play of oppositions, nuances and textures which sometimes frame the landscape, sometimes reflect it, at times modulate it and at other times subvert it. The walls of lightly coloured concrete—combined with the roughness of the limestone—the façades of marble, steel and glass, and the floors of stone, wood and water, constitute a counterpoint of complementary fragments. These, by mixing with the features of the natural landscape, extend the experience of the house to a full acknowledgement of the territory as architectural construction.

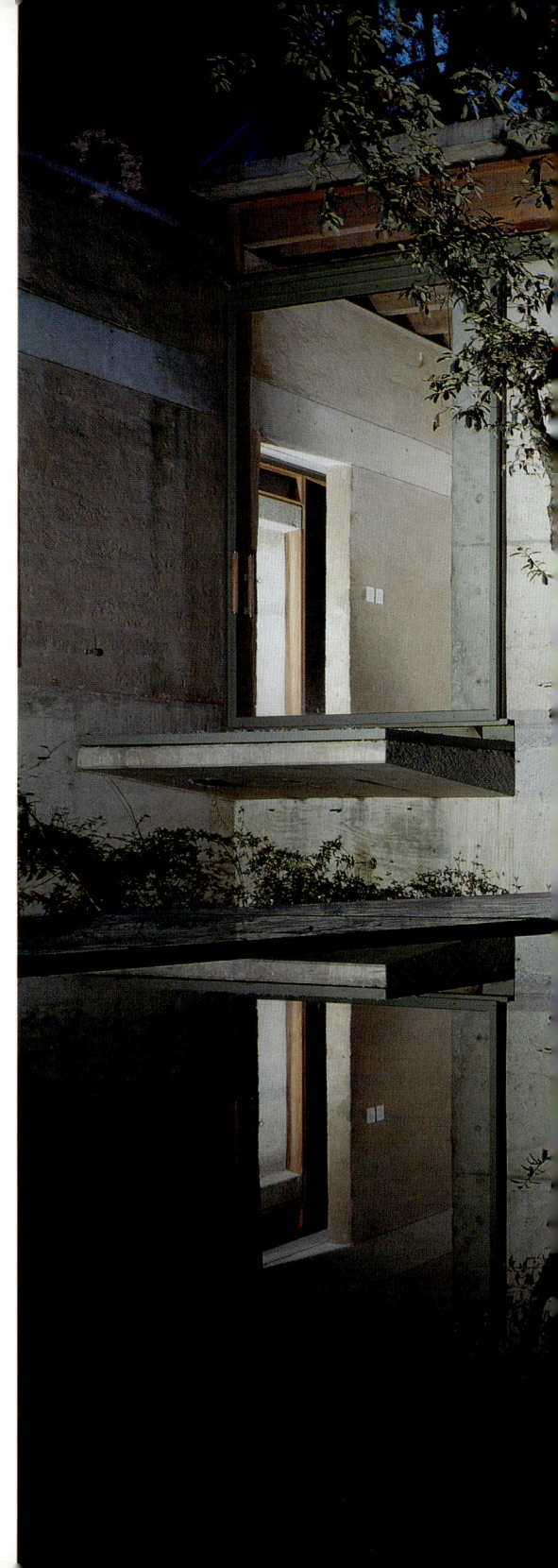

1   Sketch of the main access

Opposite page: Perspective of the swimming pool and the study at night

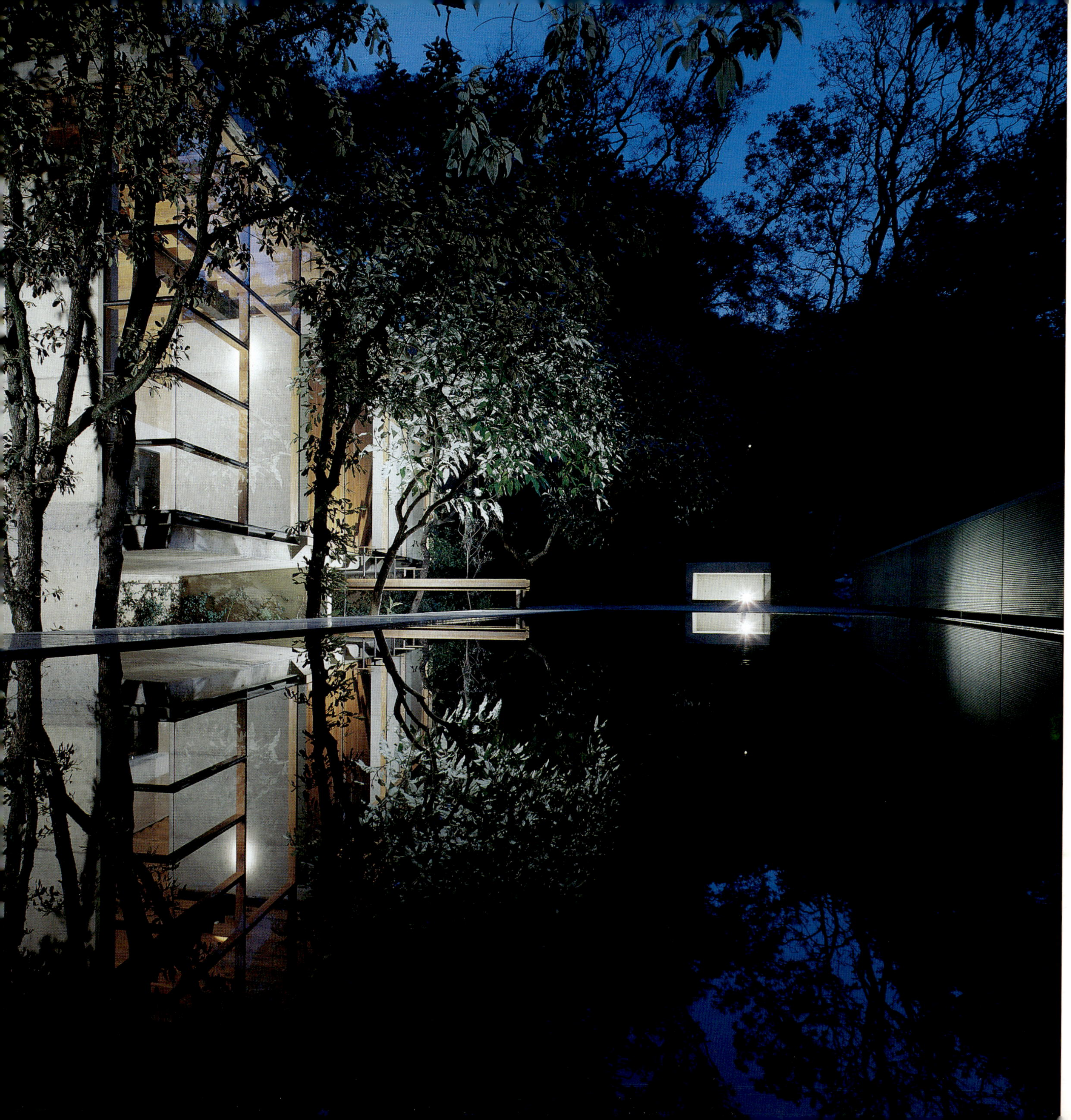

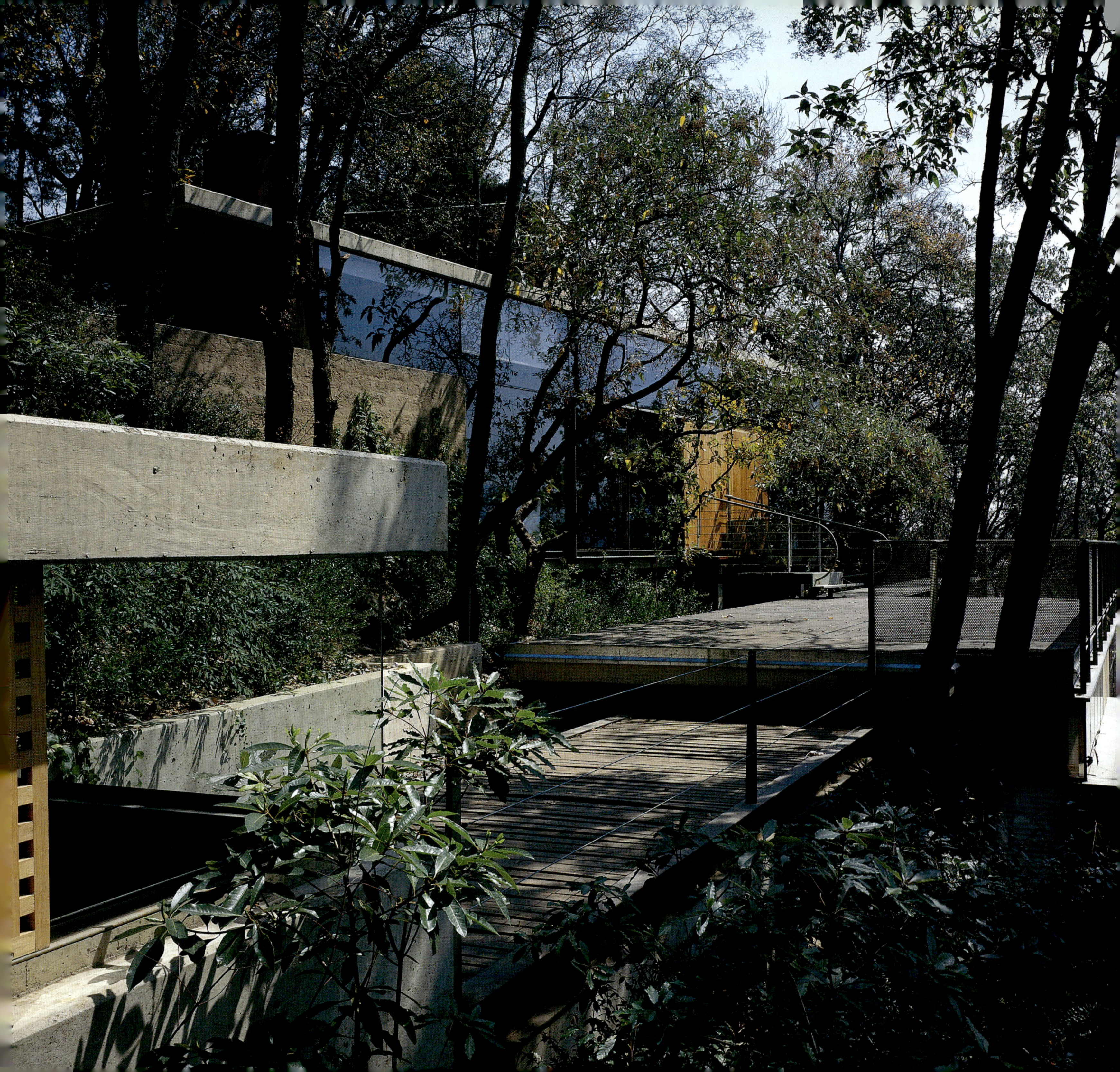

Large photo: Social areas seen from the roof and also the bedrooms
1 Site plan, sections and façades

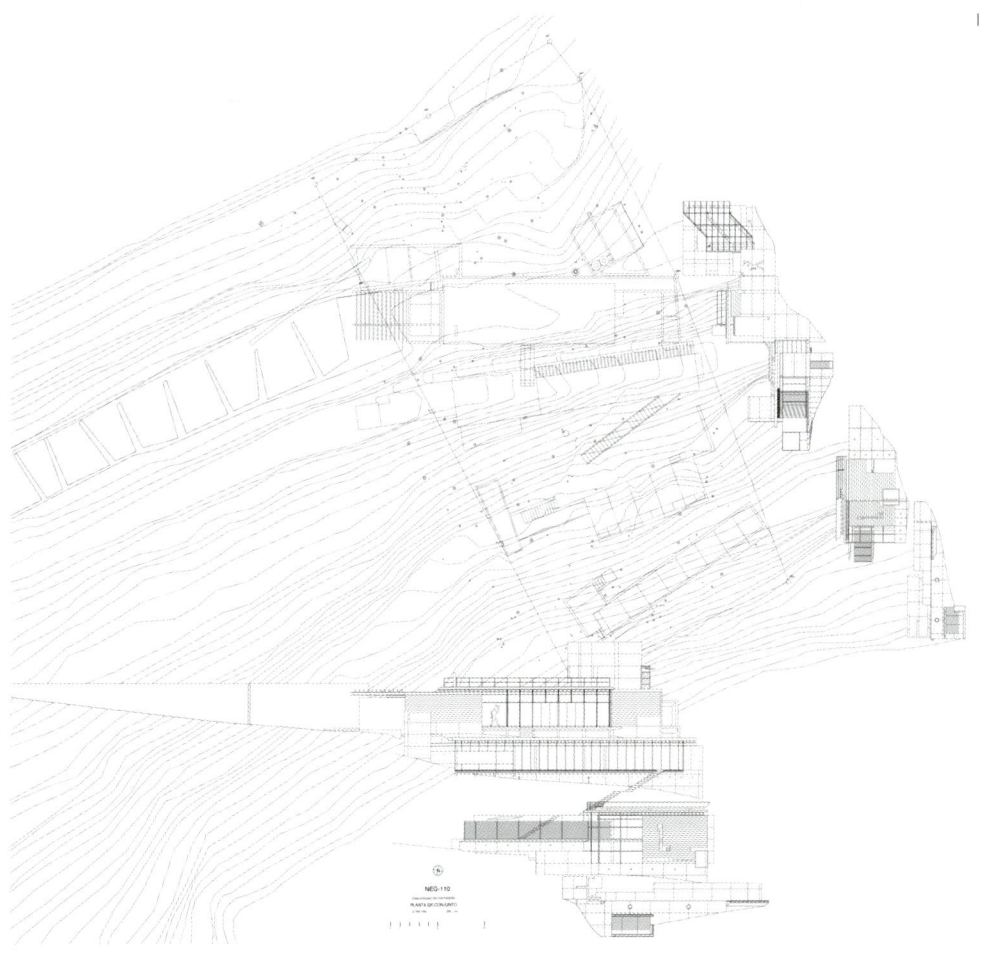

Negro House 163

1 Structural details
2 Main Access
3 Dining room

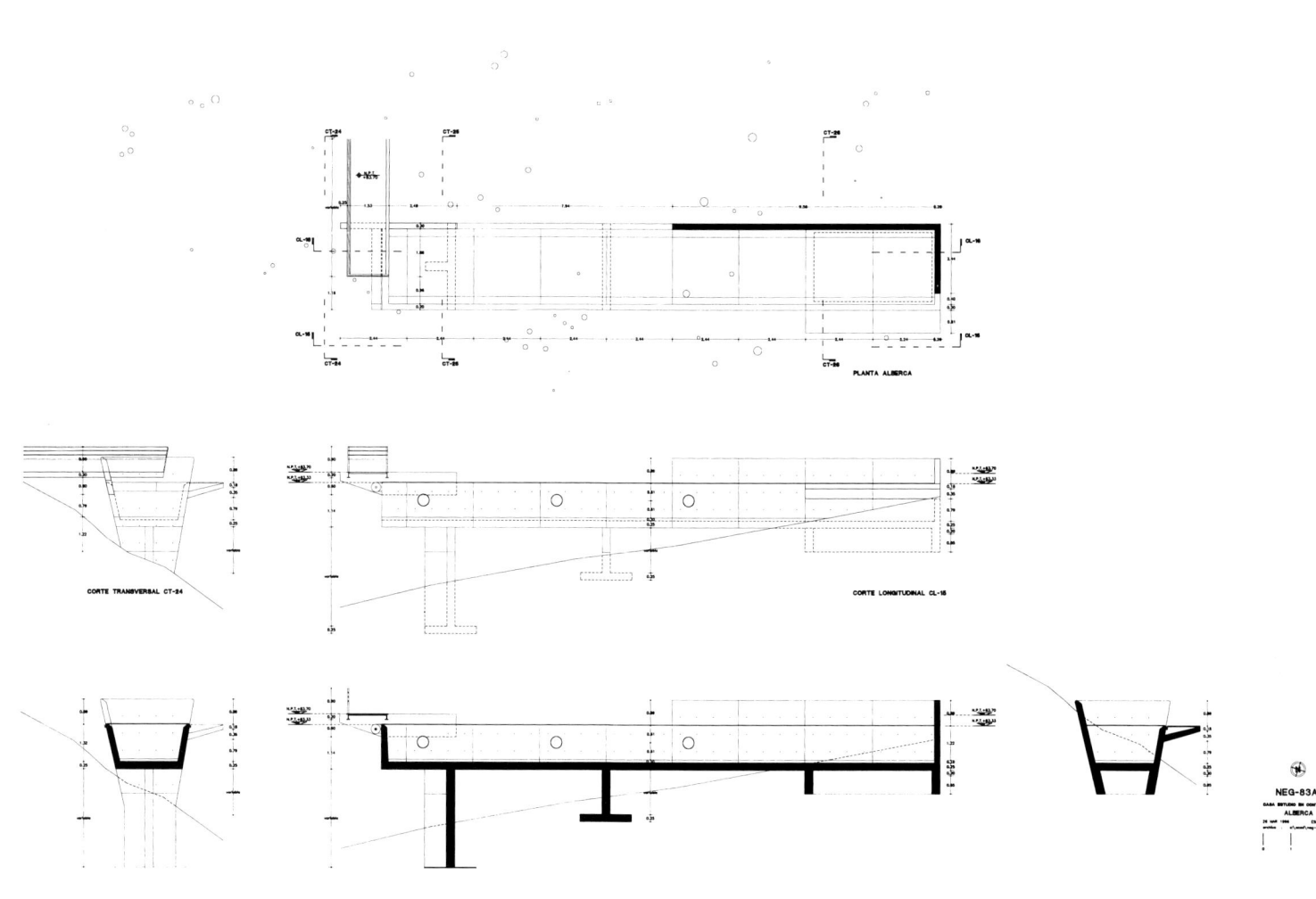

2

3

Negro House   165

Left: Access to the study area
Right: Study

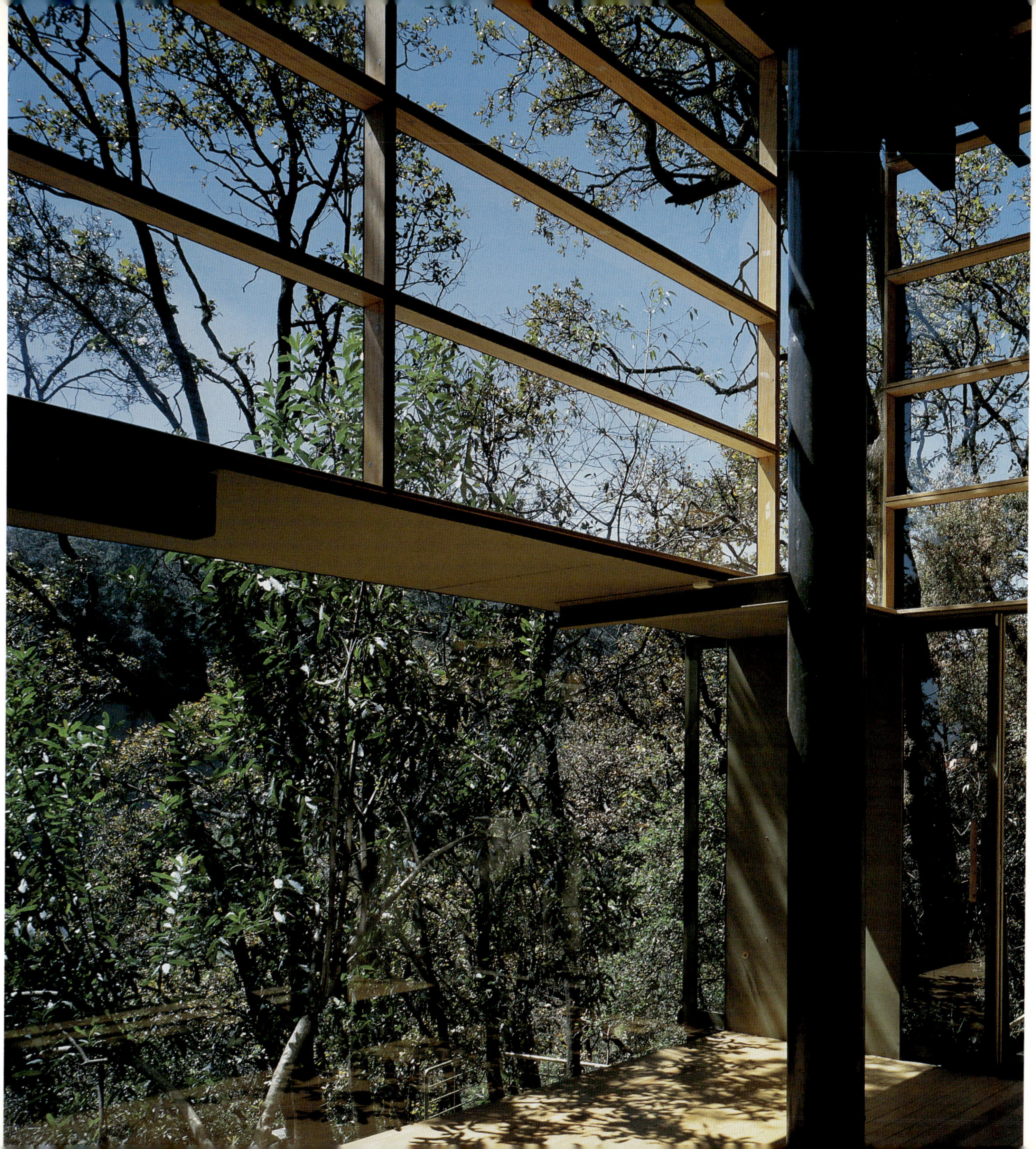

the authors

Editor's abbreviated extracts from the curricula provided by the architects themselves or their professional studios.

Jimmy Alcock

Walter James Alcock (b. 1932 Caracas, Venezuela) graduated in the Faculty of Architecture and Town Planning of the Central University of Venezuela in 1959. He worked with Burle-Marx on the East Park project in Caracas and was later associated with the Uruguayan architect José Miguel Galia, who was established in Venezuela. His extensive body of work covers institutions, private residences and commercial premises and has been recognised with prizes and awards including Venezuela's National Prize for Architecture (1997), the National Prize for the best Single-family Dwelling for his La Ribereña House, the Metropolitan Prize for the Crystal Park Building, and the Regional Prize (with Manuel Fuentes) for the Jirahara Hotel in Barquisimeto. Member of the Academy of Engineering and Dwellings of Venezuela, he has been a teacher in the Central University of Venezuela and the Simón Bolívar University, Caracas. He represented his country at the 1993 Venice Biennial.

Andrade and Morettin

Vinicius Hernandes de Andrade (b. 1968, Sao Paulo, Brazil) graduated from the School of Architecture and Town Planning, University of Sao Paulo in 1992.
After working with Paulo Mendes da Rocha in Sao Paulo and Emili Donato in Barcelona, among others, he founded Andrade Morettin Associates in 1997.
Marcelo H. Morettin (b. 1969, Sao Paulo) graduated also from the Sao Paulo School of Architecture and Town Planning (1991) and then worked with Joaquim Gedes. Andrade and Morettin have received many prizes and awards, including the First Prize in a National Competition for the restoration of the Medical School of the University of Sao Paulo (1998) and the Award for Young Architects promoted by IAB in the Casa Brasileira Museum. Their work has been widely exhibited: e.g. *Brazil still Builds – Brazilian Houses*, at the Architectural Association of London, and at the XIX Congress of the International Union of Architects in Barcelona (1996).

Renato Luiz Sobral Anelli

(B. 1959, Campinas, Sao Paulo, Brazil). Graduate from the Faculty of Architecture and Town Planning of the Catholic Pontifical University of Campinas (1982), Master's degree in History from the Institute of Philosophy and Human Sciences of the University of Campinas (1990), and doctorate from the Faculty of Architecture and Town Planning of the University of Sao Paulo (1995).
From 1994 to 1995 and in 1998 he undertook research in the University Institute of Architecture of Venice. He has been teacher in the Department of Architecture and Town Planning at the School of Engineering at Sao Carlos, Sao Paulo University, since 1986, where he teaches Project courses for undergraduates and History for postgraduate students. He was head of Department between March 1999 and December 2000. Since January 2001 he has been Municipal Secretary of Public Works and Services of the City of Sao Carlos.

Benjamín Barney-Caldas

(B. 1941, Cali, Colombia). Graduated as an architect from the University of the Andes in Bogotá (1967), where he later became teacher and researcher, as well as at the Centre for Aesthetic Research and at the Centre for Urban Planning (1968-72). He was teacher in the University of the Valley (1972-97), director of his old School of Architecture and of the Higher Institute of Architecture and Design of Chihuahua, Mexico (2000). His projects have been published in Colombia, Italy and Uruguay, and his La Queja House was named for the Mies van der Rohe Architecture Prize for Latin America (2000). He is a columnist for the newspaper *El País* of Cali, and co-author with F. Ramírez of *La arquitectura de las casas de hacienda en el Valle del Alto Cauca*, 1994, and (with others) of *Patrimonio Urbano en Colombia*, 1996, and of *Estudios sobre el territorio iberoamericano*, 1996. He was vice-president of the Colombian Society of Architects, Del Valle branch (1993-98.)

Agrait y Betancourt

Carlos E. Betancourt Llambias graduated from the University of Puerto Rico's School of Architecture, with a Master's degree in Architecture (1978). He is a member of the American Institute of Architects (AIA), Puerto Rico branch. In 1985 he formed his own firm of architecture which has since won prizes in several forums: the Premier Prize of Honour for non-constructed architecture at the Biennial of the Puerto Rico College of Architecture for the project for the Museum of Natural History of Puerto Rico in 1996, a project which also won an award from the American Institute of Architects in Florida. In 1999 his House on the Lake received the Premier Prize of Honour from the American Institute of Architects of Puerto Rico and the College of Architects of this institute awarded him the Prize of Honour at the V Biennial. Since 1985 he has been Teacher of Design at the School of Architecture of the Polytechnic University of Puerto Rico.

Cristian Boza

Gained a diploma in Architecture from the Catholic University of Chile in 1968, and a diploma in Urban Design and Planning from the University of Edinburgh in 1971. He was teacher at the University of Development in Santiago (1999-2001). Since 1985 Cristian Boza & Associate Architects have built 800,000 sq. metres of dwellings, offices and commercial premises. His work has been exhibited in a monograph at the University of Development in Santiago (2000). He has attended numerous conferences in the Americas, Britain, France and Spain. He has won a good number of first prizes in competitions, such as those for the urban development of Vilumanque, Concepción in 1999, Serena Norte, 1999, and Pudahuel New City, Santiago, 1996-97. Another award was the Quito Biennial Prize for the Manhattan office building in Santiago, 1995. He is author of half a dozen books including *100 años de arquitectura en Chile*, 1996, as well as of numerous articles.

Enrique Browne

(B. 1942, Santiago, Chile). First degree in Architecture, 1965, and Master's in Town Planning, 1988, from the Catholic University of Chile. He has followed advanced courses in England and Japan. Scholarships from the Ford Foundation in 1969, the Guggenheim in 1984, and from the Social Science Research Council in 1975. He has won numerous prizes in competitions and architecture biennials including first prizes in the Biennials of Chile in 1979 and 1995, the Silver Medal at the World Biennial of Architecture in Sofia, Bulgaria, 1989, and the First Prize for Latin America in Buenos Aires, 1998. He was short-listed in the I Ibero-American Biennial in Madrid, 1998, and the Vitruvio Prize at the I International Biennial of Art (Buenos Aires, 2000). He is author of *Otra Arquitectura en América Latina*, 1988, and of some 50 essays. Three monographs on his work have been published, as well as some 150 magazine articles. He has attended conferences in the USA, Latin America and Europe.

Mariano Clusellas

(B. 1963, Buenos Aires, Argentina). He is graduate in Architecture from the University of Buenos Aires (UBA), 1989; attended conferences and classes at the Fine Arts Museum in Houston and the Faculty of Architecture and Town Planning, UBA. Assistant to professor Horacio Baliero, University Di Tella, Buenos Aires, and to the architects Dahl-Rocha and José Cruz in the Catholic Pontifical University of Santiago. His writings have been published in magazines and daily newspapers in Argentina (*Sunma, Sunma +, Living, Clarín, La Nación*), Chile (*ARQ*), Spain (*2G*) and Mexico (*ARQUINE*). Among his most recent work, in addition to offices, are numerous unifamily houses, such as the Colle, Levinson, Camorino, Royo, the Cambre house-studio and the interior of the Kuitca house—Buenos Aires—the Taraciuk, Secreto and Susevich houses, the rural house of La Arenisca, the House in La Barranca and a viewing tower on the River Plate—Colonia, Uruguay.

Ignacio Dahl-Rocha

A Yale University graduate, he has also studied in the University of Buenos Aires (UBA) and at the Graduate School of Design at Harvard University. He has taken part in various seminars in Europe and Latin America. Since 1990 he has practised his profession in Switzerland in partnership with Jacques Richter at the offices of Richter et Dahl-Rocha Bureau d'Architectes SA. Up to 1989 he was the senior member of the firm Billoch / Dahl-Rocha / Ramos which he formed along with Francisco Billoch and Juan Ignacio Ramos, fellow graduates from the Faculty of Architecture and Town Planning of the UBA (1978).

His work has attracted much attention, both through exhibitions and publications, in the United States, Latin America, and Europe, and he was finalist for the first edition of the Palladio Prize in Venice in 1988. He also received the Prize of the Buenos Aires Biennial in 1989.

Alejandro Echeverri R. / Juan Bernardo Echeverri C.

A partnership formed in 1990, both architects are graduates of the Bolivarian Pontifical University in Medellin, where they have been teaching since 1994. In 1989 Juan B. gained a diploma in Architecture from the London Architectural Association. Alejandro got his doctorate from the University of Barcelona in 1989. Among their numerous awards are: the National Prize for Architecture at the XV Colombian Biennial of Architecture in Santafé de Bogota in 1996, for the Posada House, with which they also obtained an Honourable Mention in Architectonic Design by the X Panamerican Biennial of Architecture, at Quito, Ecuador in 1996. They have entered many competitions and have had their work shown not only at biennials but in exhibitions at the Lepold Rother Museum of Architecture, the National University of Colombia at Santafé de Bogotá, 2000; the Museum of Modern Art, Medellin, 1999; the Museum of Modern Art the Tertulia of Cali, etc.

Teodoro González de León

(B. 1926, Mexico City). He studied at the Academy of San Carlos (1942-1947, UNAM). A scholarship from the French government took him to work for 18 months with Le Corbusier (1947-48), when he supervised the programme for the Housing Unit in Marseilles and the Manufacturing Plant of St. Dié. Since his return to Mexico he has been engaged in town planning, popular housing schemes and large buildings in the public and the private sector. It is impossible to summarise here his extensive work, individually or in co-operation with Zabludovsky—Mexico College, the Rufino Tamayo Museum—and Francisco Serrano. He has won the highest prizes in Latin America; Grand Prize of the International Academy of Architecture at the Sofia Biennial, in 1989 and in 1994. Honorary Member of the American Institute of Architects, his work has been on exhibition in museums in Mexico, Madrid, Barcelona, Pamplona and widely published in books and magazines.

Rafael Iglesia

(B. 1952, Concordia, Entre Rios, Argentina). He is a graduate in Architecture from the Faculty of Architecture, Planning and Design at the National University of Rosario (1981). He was Silver Medallist at the World Forum of Young Architects at the International Biennial of Architecture in Buenos Aires 1991. He won the First Prize at Emergent Voices, Buenos Aires International Biennial of Architecture in 1989. He received the Mies van der Rohe Award for Latin American Architecture in 2000 for La Barranca House in Paraná, Arroyo Seco, which also won the Roca Prize, by the daily *Cronista Comercial* of Buenos Aires in 2000. His housing projects include the house in calle Juana Azurduy, Buenos Aires, 1994, and the Genera House in Fisherton, Rosario, 2000. The CONYSTAR building in Rosario (1999) is one of his works and he has designed telephone booths for Telecom, as well as a cardiovascular clinic, nursery schools, commercial premises and industrial sites.

Carlos Jiménez

(B. 1959, San Jose, Costa Rica). He moved to the US in 1974. After graduation from the School of Architecture of the University of Houston in 1981, he opened his own offices in Houston in 1982. He has taught at several universities: Rice, Texas; Southern California Institute of Architecture, UCLA; Arlington, Texas; Houston, Texas; Williams College; Navarra; Harvard; Tulane; Austin, Texas; Berkeley; Oregon. He was a member of the Pritzker Prize jury (2000) and a conference speaker in the USA, Canada, Italy, Spain, Switzerland and Latin America. Numerous prizes from US institutions.

His work has been shown in museums and related centres in Houston, New York, Los Angeles, Montreal, Santa Monica, Austin, Mexico, Manhattan-Kansas, Williamstown, New Orleans, Fort Worth, Chicago, Cambridge, Arrecife in Lanzarote (Canary Islands), Kansas City, and has been the subject of six books (New York 1996; Barcelona 1991).

Paulo Archias Mendes da Rocha

(B. 1928, Vitoria, Espirito Santo, Brazil). Graduation and diploma from the Faculty of Architecture and Town Planning Mackenzie University (1954). Since 1960 he has taught in the Faculty of Architecture and Town Planning, University of Sao Paulo. Since 1957 he has won first prizes in competitions for his designs—all constructed. He won the President of the Republic's Grand Prize at the VI International Biennial of Sao Paulo (1961) and attended the Venice Biennial (1986 and 2000) and the Havana Biennial (1994). He was a guest at the X Kassel Documenta, at the *Anybody Conference* in Buenos Aires, 1996, and at the *Less is More* of the UIA Congress of Barcelona 1996. Winner of the Latin American Grand Prize at the X Biennial of Architecture, Santiago, 1995, and Prizes for Life-time Achievements at the I Ibero-American Biennial of Architecture, Madrid, 1998; Ministry of Culture, Brazil, 1998; Mies van der Rohe Prize for Latin American Architecture, Barcelona, 2000.

Alberto Kalach

(B. 1960, Mexico City). He studied Architecture in the Ibero American University of Mexico (1977-81) and the Cornell University, New York (1983-1985). He has won many first prizes in open competitions and was chosen for the Elliot Noyes Chair at Harvard University Graduate School of Design in 1998. His work has been exhibited collectively: in Mexico—Museum of Modern Art, Sloane Gallery, Museum of Fine Arts, Racota, Carrillo Gil Museum—in New York—Columbia University, Storefront Gallery—and Los Angeles—California University—and individually at Harvard (1999) and the Palacio of Fine Arts, Mexico (1999). He has been speaker at conferences in universities, museums and other centres in Mexico, the USA, Puerto Rico, Madrid and Paris and has taught in the Ibero American University and UNAM of Mexico, Houston, South California, Harvard. His work may be found in more than 50 publications in books and international magazines.

Leopoldo Laguinge

(B. 1955, Cordoba, Argentina). He obtained his first degree in Architecture in the Catholic University of Cordoba in 1979 and his Master's at the University of Cincinnati, USA, 1985. He began his professional career in the S.O.M. Studio in Chicago (1985-1986). Later, he joined Bohm NBBJ, at Columbus, Ohio (1986-1988). In 1989 he opened his own office, Laguinge & Associates.

He has taught in the Schools of Architecture of Cordoba, Argentina, in 1982; in the University of Cincinnati, USA, in 1984; in the International University of Cordoba, Argentina, in 1989 and 1994; and in the Washington University of St. Louis, USA, in 1997.

His research titled *Notes on Art, Technology and Science*, 1984, was carried out at the University of Cincinnati, USA, and magazines such as *Summa* and *DBZ. Deutsche Bauzeitung* have published his work.

Enrique Larrañaga

(B. 1953, Caracas, Venezuela). He graduated in Architecture from the Simon Bolivar University in 1977 and gained his Master's degree in Environmental Design at Yale University in 1983. He has taught at the Simon Bolivar University and also at universities in Buenos Aires, Syracuse, Miami, and at Cornell. He has been speaker at several national and international congresses. **Vilma Obadía** (b. 1960, Caracas) is also an architect from the Simon Bolivar University and has been teaching at the Jose Maria Vargas University. Larrañaga and Obadía have worked together since 1988 and have won awards in many competitions. Their work, from town planning to furniture, has been exhibited in museums in Caracas—Sofía Imber Contemporary Art, of Fine Arts, Alejandro Otero Visual Arts, Institute of Urban Architecture—in Washington D.C.—National Building Museum—and in universities—Syracuse, Miami, Central of Venezuela. Their work has been widely reviewed in the specialist press.

Ana Loreto

(B. 1951, Caracas). She graduated in Architecture from the Central University of Venezuela, UCV, where she has taught since 1974. She has been a teacher in the Technological Development Department at the Institute of Experimental Development in Construction of the Faculty of Architecture and Town Planning of the UCV, where she also helds research, teaching and executive posts. Her recent projects include the restoration for tourist purposes of the Ranch Las García (1995-96) and a single-family house in Choroní for Diego Texera (1995-96), the pre-project phase of the extension (second stage) to the Las Garcias Hotel, in Choroní (1996-97) and the single-family housing project in the Hatillo, "The Other Side" sector, for Antonio Llerandi (1997). Also in 1997 she carried out the renovation plan for dual family housing in La Floresta for Silvia Sánchez. In 1998 she worked on the holiday housing complex in Choroní.

TEN Architects

Enrique Norten (b. 1954, Mexico City), graduated in Architecture from the Ibero American University in Mexico in 1978. He took his teacher's degree in Architecture at Cornell University, New York, 1980. Honorary Member of the American Academy of Architects, 1999. Chairs: O'Neill Ford at the University of Texas in Austin; Elliot Noyes in Harvard; Emil Lorch in Michigan. Currently he is Miller professor at the University of Pennsylvania in Philadelphia. **Bernardo Gómez-Pimienta** (b. 1961, Brussels) got his degree in Architecture at the University of Anahuac, Mexico City in 1986 and his teaching degree at Columbia University, New York, 1987. He has taught in universities of Mexico and the US. Some of his buildings have received national and international prizes—such as the Mies van der Rohe Prize for Latin American Architecture, Barcelona 1998—and have appeared in the most prestigious international publications.

Juan Manuel Peláez

(B. 1969, Medellín, Colombia). An architect from the National University of Medellin. With a Master's in the Theory and History of Architecture from the School of Barcelona (1995-96), he has been Projects teacher since 1998 in the Bolivarian Pontifical University and in the National University of Colombia. His work, with numerous single-family houses—the Restrepo House or the Horas Claras House, both in El Retiro, Antioquía—has won several competitions—the Novotel Corali Hotel in Costa Rica, with Felipe Uribe, 2000—and has taken part in the IV International Biennial of Sao Paulo, 2000; in the XVI Biennial of Architecture, Colombia, 1998; in the XI Latin American Biennial of Architecture, Quito, Ecuador. He was a finalist for the Opera Prima *Bauwelt Prize*, Berlin 2000; First Prize in the International Competition of Architecture First Constructions / Aguirre Newman, Madrid 1998. His works have been published in books and magazines.

María de la Guardia
Teófilo Victoria

María M. de la Guardia has a Bachelor's degree in Architecture from the University of Miami (1984) and a Master's in Architecture from Harvard University.

Teófilo Victoria got his Bachelor's degree in Architecture from the Rhode Island School of Design and his Master's at Columbia University. Their many projects include dwellings as well as single-family houses, particularly at Miami Beach, Florida, as also apartment blocks, commercial centres, tourist complexes, housing for workmen in areas such as Key Biscayne, Coral Gables, Miami Beach and Rosemary Beach, Florida in Nassau and Marsh Harbor in Bahamas; Asuncion in Paraguay; Nemocon in Colombia, etc. Together with Trelles Architects they have worked on several high-rise tower blocks in Miami Beach, which have been exhibited in Brussels, Groningen, Miami, Harvard and the 1983 World Biennial in Bulgaria.

Agrait-Betancourt, C. 82, 84.1, 84.3, 84.4, 86.1, 86.2
Agrait-Betancourt, C. / Marcial, I.M. / Morales, F. S. 83, 84.2, 85.5, 86.3, 87.4, 88.1, 88.2, 89.3
Alcock, J. 146.1, 149.2, 149.5, 150.1, 150.2, 152.1
Alcock, J. / Gasparini, P. 147, 148.1, 149.3, 149.4, 150-151, 152.2, 153
Andrade, V. y Morettin, M. 110.1, 110.2, 110.3, 113.3, 113.5, 113.6
Andrade, V. y Morettin, M. / Kon, N. 111, 112.1, 112.2, 113.4, 114-115, 116-117.1, 117.2
Anelli, R. L. Sobral 126.1, 128.1, 129.3, 130
Anelli, R. L. Sobral / Carvalho e Silva, T. 126-127, 128.2, 129.4, 130-131
Archivos de Arquitectura Antillana / Moré 9.c
Barney-Caldas, B. 98.1, 100.1, 100.2, 100.4
Barney-Caldas, B / Patiño, S. 99.2, 100.3, 101.5, 102.1, 103.2, 103.3
Billocoh, F. / Dahl-Rocha, I. / Ramos, J. I. 56.1, 56.2, 58.1
Billocoh, F. / Dahl-Rocha, I. / Ramos, J. I. / Riverti, R. 54-55, 57.3, 58.2, 59.3, 60.1, 60.2, 61.3
Boza, C. 154.1, 156.1, 157.3, 158.1, 158.2
Boza, C. / Wenborne, G. 155, 156.2, 157.4, 158-159
Browne, E. 32.1, 34.1, 35.3, 35.5, 36.2
Browne, E / De la Fuente, R. 33.2, 34.2, 35.4, 36.1, 37
Clusellas, M. y Baliero, H. 74, 76.2, 76.3, 76.4, 78.2, 78.3, 78.4, 80.1
Clusellas, M. y Baliero, H. / Sosa Pinilla, G. y Chouela-Living 75, 76.1, 77.5, 78-79.1, 79.5, 80.2, 81
Colección Fundación Galería de Arte Nacional / Gasparini, P. 13.b
Colección Patricia Phelps de Cisneros 10.e
Colección Patricia Phelps de Cisneros / Barros, A. 11.a
Colección Museo de Bellas Artes, Caracas 9.g, 11.b, 12.b, 12.g, 13.a
De la Guardia, V. Architects 68, 70.2, 70.3
De la Guardia, V. Architects / Southern Living, Martín, S. Photographer 69, 70.1, 71, 72.1, 72.2, 73.3
Echeverri Arquitectos 132.1, 132.2, 134.1, 134.2
Echeverri Arquitectos / Echeverri, A. 133, 134-135.3, 136.1, 136.2, 137.3
González de León, T. 138, 141.2, 141.3, 142.1
González de León, T. / Gordoa, L. 138-139, 140-141, 144.1, 144.2, 145.3
González de León, T. / Hiriart, P. 142.2, 143.3
Iglesia, R. 118.1, 118.2, 118.3, 121.2, 122.1, 122.2
Iglesia, R. / Frittegotto, G. 119, 120.1, 121.3, 122.3, 123, 124, 125
Instituto Lina Bo e P. M. Bardi / Pappalardo, A 10.a
Jiménez, C. Estudio 46.1, 46.2, 48.2, 48.3, 48.4, 48.5, 50.1
Jiménez, C. Estudio / Hester, P., Hester+Hodaway Photographers 47, 48.1, 49.6, 50.2, 51.3, 52.1, 52.2, 53
Kalach, A., Alvarez, D. 160.1, 163.1, 164.1
Kalach, A., Alvarez, D. / Gordoa, L., Czitrom, P., Alcántara, M. I. 160-161, 162-163, 165.2, 165.3, 166, 167
Laguinge, L. 62.1, 62.2, 64.1, 64.2, 64.3, 66.1
Laguinge, L. / Pérez, A. 63, 65, 66-67.2
Larrañaga, E. 8.b, 8.c, 10.b, 10.d, 11.c, 12.e, 13.c, 13.f, 97
Larrañaga, E. / Gasparini, G. 8.d, 8.e, 8.f, 9.a, 9.b, 9.d, 9.e, 9.f, 11.d, 12.a, 13.d, 13.e
Larrañaga, E. / Obadía, V. 90, 92.2, 94.1, 94.2
Larrañaga, E. / Obadía, V. / Iacobelli, A. 91, 93, 94.3, 95, 96-97
Larrañaga, E. / Obadía, V. / Armas, R. 92.1
Larrañaga, E. / Oquet, C. 12.c
Larrañaga, E. / Stiuv, R. 12.f
Larrañaga, E. / Tenrreiro, O. 8.a
Loreto, A. 104.1, 104.2, 104.3, 106.2, 107.3, 108.1
Loreto, A. / Brito, L., Marcano, G. 105, 106.1, 107.4, 108.2, 109.3
Mendes Da Rocha, P. 16.1, 16.2, 16.3, 22.1
Mendes Da Rocha, P. / Yendo, C. 17, 18.1, 18-19, 20-21, 22.2, 23
Peláez, J. M. 38.1, 38.2, 40.1, 40.2, 40.3, 40.4, 40.5, 41.6, 43.1, 43.2, 43.3
Peláez, J. M. / Peláez Freidel, J.M. 39, 41.7, 42-43, 44.1, 44.2, 45.3
Schneider Gallery y Sicardi Gallery 12.d
Tanais Ediciones / Lagrange, F. 10.c